MID-CONTINENT PUBLIC LIBRARY

North Independence Branch **NI**
Highway 24 & Spring
Independence, MO 64050

WITHDRAWN
FROM THE RECORDS OF THE
MID-CONTINENT PUBLIC LIBRARY

OCT 2 5

THE COMICS COME ALIVE:

A Guide to Comic-Strip Characters in Live-Action Productions

by
ROY KINNARD

The Scarecrow Press, Inc.
Metuchen, N.J., & London
1991

Frontispiece: BATMAN (Columbia, 1943): Lewis Wilson in the title role.

MID-CONTINENT PUBLIC LIBRARY

3 0000 10711590 3

Ref
791.43652
K622

MID-CONTINENT PUBLIC LIBRAR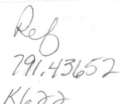

North Independence ~ ..cn
Highway 24 & Spring
Independence, MO 64050

British Library Cataloguing-in-Publication data available

Library of Congress Cataloging-in-Publication Data

Kinnard, Roy, 1952–
    The comics come alive : a guide to comic-strip characters in
live-action productions / by Roy Kinnard.
        p.   cm.
    Includes bibliographical references and index.
    ISBN 0-8108-2409-4 (acid-free paper)
    1. Comic strip characters in motion pictures.   I. Title.
PN1995.9.C36K56   1991
791.43'652—dc20   91-16890

Copyright © 1991 by Roy Kinnard
Manufactured in the United States of America

Printed on acid-free paper

CONTENTS

ACKNOWLEDGMENTS

I would like to thank the following individuals for contributing information and materials to this book: Tony Clay; Phyllis Coates; Buster Crabbe (deceased); Fred Palkovics; Jean Rogers; Penny Singleton; Brian Stagg; Veto Stasiunaitus; Richard Vitone; Tom Weaver.

Very special thanks are also extended to these individuals, for their extraordinary generosity and invaluable assistance: Ed Bernds; Tim Davis; Jim Shoenberger; George Turner.

Roy Kinnard
Chicago, IL

INTRODUCTION

The concept of the newspaper syndicate began in 1841 when Moses Y. Beach of the *New York Sun* published several printed copies of a political speech and sold these pre-printed accounts to various local papers. Within a few years, the *New York Sun* was selling entire sections of pre-printed news to other newspapers. In 1861, Ansel Nash Kellogg bought syndicated news material from the *Wisconsin State Journal* for his own paper, the *Baraboo Republican*. This inspired the *Wisconsin State Journal* to begin the first regular syndication of newspaper material, which in turn prompted Kellogg to found the first true newspaper syndicate, the A. N. Kellogg News Co., which he began in 1865, distributing various gags and features. Up to this point, most syndication activity had been small-time, but a few years later in the 1880s, big business entered the picture when Irving Bacheller originated the New York Press Syndicate, distributing interviews with the important newsmakers of the day to major papers. The *New York Sun* began national syndication of fictional material, and the *New York World* sold material by humorist Bill Nye and cartoonist Walt McDougall to various papers around the country. S. S. McClure began his own syndicate in 1884, and by the mid-1890s, the syndicated newspaper comic strip was born, with omnipotent newsprint barons like William Randolph Hearst and his competitor Joseph Pulitzer entering and quickly dominating the field.

By 1915, Hearst had combined several distribution operations into King Features Syndicate. The NEA Service was founded by Robert Paine of the *Cleveland Press* in 1901. In 1907 George Matthew Adams created the George Matthew Adams Service, which was ultimately bought by the Washington Star Syndicate. V. V. McNitt, who had begun the *Central*

Press of Cleveland in 1910 and sold it to Hearst, began the Associated Newspapers Syndicate in 1912 and the McNaught Syndicate in 1922, both of which were then combined and absorbed by United Features Syndicate. John Wheeler began the Bell Syndicate, and the Ledger Syndicate was formed in 1915. In 1919 the *Chicago Tribune*'s Joseph M. Patterson started the Chicago Tribune–New York News Syndicate, and the same year Eugene P. Cowley began Associated Editors. In 1925 Cowley and H. H. Anderson formed Publishers Syndicate, which was later absorbed (along with the Hall Syndicate) by Field Enterprises.

The subject matter of the various comic strips distributed by these syndicates covered a wide range: detective/mystery (DICK TRACY, SECRET AGENT X–9); fantasy/science fiction (BUCK ROGERS, FLASH GORDON, BRICK BRADFORD); historical (PRINCE VALIANT); adventure (TERRY AND THE PIRATES); and romantic/adventure (BRENDA STARR), but most of the strips were, and remain to this day, humorous in nature (BLONDIE, GASOLINE ALLEY). Aside from a few excursions into the realm of science fiction, such as FLASH GORDON, the more fantastic comic-strip characters were to be found in comic books.

In 1933, publisher Max C. Gaines, having seen a 7″ × 9″ Sunday comics section printed by the Ledger Syndicate, hit upon the idea of distributing comic strips in booklet form, and published FUNNIES ON PARADE, a collection of newspaper-strip reprints. If one passes over a few scattered attempts at selling newsstand reprints of strips in the previous decades, this was the first comic book, designed as a promotional giveaway for Procter and Gamble. Gaines was soon publishing FAMOUS FUNNIES: A CARNIVAL OF COMICS, and CENTURY COMICS, both containing newspaper-strip reprint material, then FAMOUS FUNNIES and SKIPPY'S OWN BOOK OF COMICS (featuring the Percy Crosby character). In 1935 National Periodical Publications published NEW FUN (the title of which was changed to MORE FUN after issue #6). This was the first standard-sized comic book to publish original material.

Soon, a number of other publishers were entering the field, and in June of 1938, National Periodical Publications debuted the standard-bearer of the comic-book industry, Superman, in ACTION COMICS #1, and in May of the next year Batman first appeared in DETECTIVE COMICS #27. Today, National Periodical Publications is known as DC Comics, drawing its corporate initials from the title of DETECTIVE COMICS.

Myriad superhero characters, all of them derivatives of Superman and Batman in one way or another, flourished in the '30s and '40s, only to decline in popularity as the industry itself did in the postwar years. In 1954, with the publication of Dr. Fredric Wertham's book *Seduction of the Innocent*, comic books were criticized by educators and politicians for their allegedly negative influence on American youth. With the United States Senate sub-committee on juvenile delinquency investigating comics (spurred on by the graphic violence in some horror titles), the major publishers in the field created the Comics Code Authority, a self-censoring board that stifled creativity and freedom of expression in the industry. Nevertheless, the formation of the Comics Code Authority in all probability saved the industry from government censorship at a time when it was under serious attack from all sides.

In 1956, National Periodicals began a revival of its superhero line, and in 1961 Stan Lee introduced the popular Marvel Comics characters with the appearance of the THE FANTASTIC FOUR, and, the following year, SPIDER-MAN. Lee and his creative stable of artists, including Jack Kirby and Steve Ditko, breathed new life into a dying industry, and a veritable comic-book renaissance was under way.

Comic books gained in popularity and appeal during the '60s and '70s, until a gradual decline in sales, resulting in part from over-production, began to cripple the industry in the late '70s and early '80s. The rise of direct sales distribution—the sale of comic books through specialty shops instead of traditional newsstand distribution—once again saved the industry, but, even though the long-overdue abandonment of the Comics Code Authority freed artists and writers from restrictive censorship, comic books were now "special interest" publications appealing to a very minor segment of the population, and no longer the mass medium they once were.

Since the introduction of the newspaper comic strip and the comic book, purveyors of entertainment in other media have been eager to adapt comic-strip characters, sensing the obvious profits to be earned from a pre-sold audience already familiar with the material. Broadway musicals such as *Annie* (adapted from the newspaper strip LITTLE ORPHAN ANNIE) are not an exclusively modern phenomenon; there were theatrical adaptations of comic strips like BRINGING UP FATHER in the early years of the century, and motion-picture adaptations were not far behind.

Comic-strip adaptations have spanned all the media, including theater and radio, but movies and television have produced the most strip adaptations, since they are primarily visual forms that accommodate both simple sight gags and elaborate visual effects far more easily than theater and radio, and also since movies and television, like the comics themselves, have always sought the widest possible audience. Although there have been hundreds of animated cartoon adaptations of comic strips, and there are many laudable and finely crafted examples, such as the lushly delineated Max Fleischer POPEYE and SUPERMAN cartoons, far more interesting are the live-action movie and television adaptations of comic strips.

No matter how well-animated the result may be, it is relatively simple to *draw* an imaginative character like Superman, but how can that same pen-and-ink creation, with only simple drawings for inspiration, be represented by a live actor? And is there enough money in the budget, and are the technicians involved resourceful enough, to represent him properly at all? Often, the answer in both cases was negative. Many of the live-action adaptations of comic strips were relegated, appropriately enough, to the movie serials, which were the film equivalent of the comic strips. Produced quickly and cheaply on tight budgets, and denied by their lowly status in the industry access to the opulent studio production facilities available to top-of-the-line "A" features, serials were, more often than not, disappointing. They were disappointing not just because they were cheap, but because their creators, resigned to the fact that their tacky little productions would be seen only at matinees by an audience consisting largely of children, didn't bother to try. There were noteworthy exceptions, such as the Buster Crabbe FLASH GORDON serials, and several of the chapterplays produced by Republic Pictures, but for the most part, quality serials were few and far between.

If performers on their way up (or, more tragically, on their slide down) appeared in a serial, their future in the Hollywood film industry was grim, to say the least. Edward Bernds, a future writer and director who worked as a sound recordist at Columbia Pictures in the '30s and '40s, served time as audio technician on the Columbia serial MANDRAKE, THE MAGI-CIAN (1939), one of that studio's worst serials. Bernds remembers the film's leading man, Warren Hull, as a warm, friendly, and very talented actor, and Hull certainly displayed that talent in the serial THE SPIDER'S WEB (1938) for the same studio, but Hull's career never advanced beyond this level. "I don't care who the actor was, or how talented he was," Bernds told this writer, "I don't care if he was as good as Olivier—if he did serials, he was through." Warren Hull ended his career hosting a television game show. FLASH GORDON star Buster Crabbe told this writer, in a 1981 interview, that he was certain by the time he appeared in FLASH GORDON'S TRIP TO MARS (1938), the second serial in the series, that his prospects in Hollywood would not improve, and despite the fact that he was quite an acceptable actor, he remained in serials and "B" movies. Other performers, such as the stoic and one-dimensional Tom Tyler (the leading man in THE ADVEN-TURES OF CAPTAIN MARVEL and THE PHANTOM), performed in serials simply because they were so untalented (offering little more than an imposing physique) that they *couldn't* advance.

Significantly, comic strips dealing in fantastic (and therefore "risky") subject matter, such as FLASH GORDON and SUPERMAN, were adapted as serials, while the "safer" humorous strips, such as BLONDIE, were adapted as "B" features, which, while generally dismissed by critics, were at least a step up from the serials in prestige and budget. Television, much more so than movies, has been surprisingly cavalier in its treatment of comic strips, the resulting productions sometimes bearing little, if any, resemblance to the original strips. This is odd since television, with the widest audience of any entertainment form, would seem to be the ideal medium for the live-action adaptation of comic strips. But TV versions of characters like Captain America have been inept and instantly forgettable; only the television incarnations of Superman and Batman, each of them in quite different ways, have left an enduring mark on popular culture.

To date, many books have been written on animated cartoons (including those based on comic strips), but little attempt has been made to catalog the live-action films based on comics. The following compendium of live-action comic-strip characters in movies and television reads like a history of those media, with the films and TV shows examined reaching from the silent era to modern big-budget epics and cable-TV productions. This book deals only with American and British live-action adaptations of comic strips. The comic-strip character headings are arranged alphabetically, with newspaper-strip or comic-book origins indicated. The movie and TV adaptations of each strip are listed chronologically. Since exact release dates for movies are sometimes at variance (especially in the case of short subjects), the reader is advised that films under the same character heading released in the same year (such as the 1937 shorts listed under the heading for JOE PALOOKA) are arranged *alphabetically* within that year of release. British (*GB*) and alternate (*a.k.a.*) film titles are also indicated. Included are production credits and cast listings, followed by individual commentaries which outline the origins of the comic strips the films are based on as well as occasional brief critiques of these film and television adaptations. A word about excluded titles:

only those characters that *originated* as comic strips are included here. Thus, although THE LONE RANGER, as an example, was indeed a comic strip before adaptation to live-action film, the character was *originally from a radio program later adapted by the comics* and is therefore excluded from this study, as are countless similar inverse adaptations, including the many comic books that have in turn been adapted from movies and TV shows.

References

Barbour, Alan G. *Cliffhanger.* New York: A & W Publishers, Inc., 1977.

Horn, Maurice, ed. *The World Encyclopedia of Comics.* New York: Avon Books, 1976.

Overstreet, Robert M. *The Comic Book Price Guide.* New York: Harmony Books, annual.

ACE DRUMMOND
newspaper strip

ACE DRUMMOND (Universal, 1936—theatrical serial; 13 chapters, approximately 20 minutes each.

Credits: Associate Producers: Barney A. Sarecky, Ben Koenig; Directors: Ford Beebe, Cliff Smith; Screenplay: Wyndham Gittens, Ray Trampe, Norman S. Hall; Camera: Richard Fryer; Supervising Editor: Saul A. Goodkind; Editors: Alvin Todd, Edward Todd, Louis Sackin; Lyrics and Music (for the song "Give Me a Ship and a Song"): Kay Kellogg.

Cast: John King (Ace Drummond); Jean Rogers (Peggy Trainor); Noah Beery, Jr. (Jerry); Guy Bates Post (Grand Lama); Arthur Loft (Chang-Ho; Chester Gan (Kai-Chek); Jackie Morrow (Billy Meredith); James B. Leong (Henry Kee); James Eagle (Johnny Wong); Selmer Jackson (Meredith, Sr.); Robert Warwick (Winston); Montague Shaw (Trainor); Frederick Vogeding (Bauer); Al Bridge (Wyckoff); Lon Chaney, Jr. (Ivan); Stanley Blystone (Sergei); Ed Cobb (Nicolai); Richard Wessel (Boris); Louis Vinzinot (Lotan); Sam Ash (Le Page); Hooper Atchley (Caldoni).

Chapter Titles: (1) Where East Meets West; (2) The Invisible Enemy; (3) The Doorway of Doom; (4) The Radio Riddle; (5) Bullets of Sand; (6) Evil Spirits; (7) The Trackless Trail; (8) The Sign in the Sky; (9) Secret Service; (10) The Mountain of Jade; (11) The Dragon Commands; (12) The Squadron of Death; (13) The World's Akin.

Note: A re-edited feature version was titled SQUADRON OF DOOM.

This early 1930s aviation-adventure strip was created (and allegedly written) by World War I flying ace Captain Eddie Rickenbacker, for King Features Syndicate. The artwork was by Clayton Knight. Only a middling success, the strip was discontinued in the late 1930s.

The 1936 Universal serial based on the strip is a competent but unremarkable production, using, as was the norm with Universal, an abundance of stock footage. Star John "Dusty" King, later a popular "B" western leading man, is an acceptable hero in the role of Drummond in spite of his disturbing tendency to burst into song at the slightest provocation, belting out the mediocre lyrics of "Give Me a Ship and a Song" a few times too many, and wearing out his welcome with the audience very quickly as a result. Perhaps King's rather incongruous efforts as a crooner would have been more endurable if he had been allowed to sing different tunes instead of the same song again and again, and at least bring a little variety to the score.

There is, however, a nice Far-Eastern atmosphere, not to mention able support from pretty Jean Rogers, comic relief from Noah Beery, Jr., and Lon Chaney, Jr., in the unlikely role of a villainous Mongol.

THE ADDAMS FAMILY
magazine cartoon

THE ADDAMS FAMILY (ABC, 1964–66)—TV series; 64 episodes, 30 minutes each.

Credits: Executive Producer: David Levy; Producer; Nat Perrin; Associate Producer: Harry Browar; Series Directors: Jean Yarbrough, Sidney Lanfield, Sidney Miller, Sidney Salkow, Jerry Hopper, Nat Perrin; Series Writers: Harry Winkler, Hannibal Coons, Jameson Brewer, Bill Lutz, George

ACE DRUMMOND (Universal, 1936): John King bursts into song, eliciting the bemused indifference of a nearby stewardess.

ACE DRUMMOND (Universal, 1936): Noah Beery, Jr., John King, Jean Rogers, and Jackie Morrow.

Haight, Seaman Jacobs, Ed James, Phil Leslie, Keith Fowler, Lou Huston; Music: Vic Mizzy; Music Supervision: Dave Kahn.

Cast: Carolyn Jones (Morticia Addams/Ophelia Frump); John Astin (Gomez Addams); Jackie Coogan (Uncle Fester); Ted Cassidy (Lurch); Lisa Loring (Wednesday Addams); Ken Weatherwax (Pugsley Addams); Blossom Rock (Grandmama Addams); Margaret Hamilton (Esther Frump); Felix Silla, Roger Arravo (Cousin Itt); Rolfe Sedan (Mr. Briggs); Parley Baer (Arthur J. Henson); Eddie Quillan (Horace Beesley); Allyn Joslyn (Sam Hillard); Ellen Corby (Mother Lurch); Thing (Itself).

THE ADDAMS FAMILY (NBC, 1977)—TV special; 90 minutes; color.

Credits: Executive Producer: Charles Fries; Producer: David Levy; Director: Dennis Steinmetz; Screenplay: George Tibbles; Music: Vic Mizzy.

Cast: Carolyn Jones (Morticia Addams/Ophelia Frump); John Astin (Gomez Addams); Jackie Coogan (Uncle Fester); Ted Cassidy (Lurch); Lisa Loring (Wednesday Addams); Ken Weatherwax (Pugsley Addams); Jane Rose (Grandmama Addams); Elvia Allman (Esther Frump); Felix Silla (Cousin Itt); Henry Darrow (Pancho Addams); Jennifer Surprenant (Wednesday, Jr.); Kenneth Marquis (Pugsley, Jr.).

The darkly humorous Charles Addams cartoons, created for *The New Yorker* in 1940, specialized in dry, sardonic black humor that made the ghoulish characters and subject matter all the more hilarious. ABC Television's weekly situation "comedy" adaptation of the cartoons couldn't have been further removed from Addams' original intentions. The monstrous characters of the cartoons were well visualized, but totally without any of Addams' underlying wit. This dim misfire was an almost total creative disaster, salvaged from complete ruin only by the herculean efforts of John Astin and Carolyn Jones, two genuinely talented performers who certainly deserved better.

Film director James Whale, in his black comedy THE OLD DARK HOUSE (1932), which predated the Addams cartoons by years, probably matched Addams' style of humor closer than anyone else ever has, or ever will. The ABC series, with its half-baked scripts, lack of decent plots (or even acceptable sight gags), and ham-handed music by Vic Mizzy, is the nadir of 1960s TV-sitcom inanity. Naturally, it enjoyed some degree of success, and continues on in syndication. Latter-day attempts at reviving the show were, mercifully, unproductive.

ALLY SLOPER
newspaper strip

Created by Charles Henry Ross in August of 1867 and running until it was discontinued in the 1920s, this British humor strip spawned several early films (titles unavailable).

ARCHIE
comic book
MLJ Magazines

ARCHIE (1962)—TV pilot.

Cast: John Simpson (Archie); Cheryl Holdridge (Betty).

Note: This unsold television pilot was never televised.

ARCHIE (ABC, 1976)—TV pilot; 60 minutes; color.

Credits: Executive Producer: James Komack; Producers: Perry Cross, George Yanok; Director: Robert Scheerer; Screenplay: Eric Cohen, George Yanok, Beverly Bloomberg, Peter Galley, Mickey Rose, Neil Rosen, George Tricker; Music: Stu Gardner, Larry Farrow.

Cast: Dennis Bowen (Archie Andrews); Audrey Landers (Betty Cooper); Hilary Thompson (Veronica Lodge); Mark Winkworth (Reggie Mantle); Darrel Maury (Jughead Jones); Jim Boelsen (Moose); Susan Blu (Midge); Tifni Twitchell (Big Ethel); Gordon Jump (Mr. Andrews); Byron Webster (Mr. Weatherbee); Jane Lambert (Miss Grundy); Amzie Strickland (Mrs. Lodge); Whit Bissell (Mr. Lodge); Michelle Stacy (Little Jinx); Mae Marmy (Aunt Helen); Billy Mumy (Larry); Paul Gordon (Phil).

THE ARCHIE SITUATION COMEDY MUSICAL VARIETY SHOW (ABC, 1978)—TV pilot; 60 minutes; color.

Credits: Executive Producer: James Komack; Producer: George Yanok; Director: Tom Trbovich; Screenplay: Eric Cohen, George Yanok; Music: Stu Gardner.

Cast: Dennis Bowen (Archie Andrews); Audrey Landers (Betty Cooper); Hilary Thompson (Veronica Lodge); Mark Winkworth (Reggie Mantle); Darrel Maury (Jughead Jones); Susan Blu (Midge); Jim Boelsen (Moose); Byron Webster (Mr. Weatherbee); Jane Lambert (Miss Grundy); Gordon Jump (Mr. Andrews).

Created by artist Bob Montana, insufferably wholesome teenager Archie Andrews and his friends made their first appearance in PEP COMICS #22 in December of 1941. An entire line of Archie comic books, quickly produced by anonymous hacks on an assembly line cookie-cutter basis, eventually followed.

Considering the inoffensive mediocrity of Montana's strip, its lack of success as television fodder (except in the form of badly animated Saturday morning cartoons) is surprising, especially since Archie Andrews and his entire milieu (farther removed from reality than Mickey Rooney's ANDY HARDY films ever were) are so unimaginative, so unimposing, and so uninvolving. And so bland. ARCHIE, therefore, would seem to be a natural for television, but to date the few unsold pilots listed here represent the only live-action adaptations of the strip.

BARBARELLA
magazine strip

BARBARELLA (Paramount, 1968)—theatrical feature; 98 minutes; color.

Credits: Producer: Dino De Laurentiis; Director: Roger Vadim; Screenplay: Terry Southern, Brian Degas, Claude Brule, Jean-Claude Forest, Clement Biddle Wood, Tudor Gates, Vittorio Bonicelli, Roger Vadim; Camera: Claude Renoir; Music: Bob Crewe, Charles Fox; Editor: Victoria Mercanton; Art Director: Enrico Fea.

Cast: Jane Fonda (Barbarella); John Phillip Law (Pygar); Anita Pallenberg (Black Queen); Milo O'Shea (Concierge); David Hemmings (Dildano); Marcel Marceau (Professor Ping); Ugo Tognazzi (Mark Hand); Claude Dauphin (President of Earth).

The shapely and scantily clad futuristic lady astronaut Barbarella was created by Jean-Claude Forest for the French publication *V-Magazine* in 1962.

BARBARELLA (Paramount, 1968): Jane Fonda.

The height of self-conscious, repulsive 1960s pop-art vulgarity, the 1967 feature film based on the strip is an inevitably tasteless Dino De Laurentiis production, smugly wallowing in ugly, garish art direction, and, considering the ample budget, hampered by unforgivably cheap and unconvincing special effects. What this shallow film does offer is controversial actress Jane Fonda at the peak of her physical beauty, a visual reward that compensates, at least somewhat, for this artless misfire's otherwise total lack of merit.

BARNEY GOOGLE (SNUFFY SMITH)
newspaper strip

BARNEY GOOGLE (SNUFFY SMITH)—theatrical short subjects.

The following shorts were all released by Standard Cinema Corp. Most of them were directed by Ralph H. Cedar and written by E. V. Durling.

BEEF STEAKS (1928); HORSEFEATHERS (1928); MONEY BALKS (1928); OK MNX (1928); T-BONE HANDICAP (1928); HORSE ON BARNEY (1929); JUST A STALL (1929); NEIGH, NEIGH SPARK PLUG (1929); PACE THAT THRILLS (1929); RUNNIN' THRU THE RYE (1929); SLIDE, SPARKY, SLIDE (1929); SUNSHINE'S DARK MOMENT.

HILLBILLY BLITZKRIEG (Monogram, 1942)—theatrical feature; 63 minutes (*a.k.a.* ENEMY ROUND-UP).

Credits: Producer: Edward Gross; Director: Ray Mack; Screenplay: Ray S. Harris; Camera: Marcel Le Picard; Editor: Ralph Dixon; Music: Paul Sawtell.

Cast: Bud Duncan (Snuffy Smith); Cliff Nazarro (Barney Google); Edgar Kennedy (Sergeant Gatling); Doris Linden (Julie James); Lucien Littlefield (Professor James); Alan Baldwin (Corporal Bruce); Nicolle Andre (Marlene Zara); Jimmie Dodd (Missouri); Teddy Mangean (Dinky); Jerry Jerome (Boller); Jack Carr (Hertle); Frank Austin (Luke); Manart Kipper.

PRIVATE SNUFFY SMITH (Monogram, 1942): An original trade magazine advertisement.

SNUFFY SMITH, YARD BIRD (Monogram, 1942)—
theatrical feature; 67 minutes (*a.k.a.* PRIVATE SNUFFY SMITH;
GB: SNUFFY SMITH).

Credits: Producer: Edward Gross; Director: Edward F. Cline;
Screenplay: John Gray, Jack Henley, Lloyd French, Doncho
Hall; Camera: Marcel Le Picard; Editor: Robert Crandall;
Music: Rudy Schrager; Art Direction: Richard Irvine.

Cast: Bud Duncan (Snuffy Smith); Edgar Kennedy (Sergeant
Cooper); Sarah Padden (Loweezie); Doris Linden (Cindy);
Andria Palmer (Janie); J. Farrell MacDonald (General); Pat
McVeigh (Lloyd); Frank Austin (Saul); Jimmie Dodd (Don).

Created by Billy De Beck for King Features Syndicate, this
long-running humor strip originally appeared under the title
MARRIED LIFE in the *Chicago Herald* in 1916. In the early
installments, Barney Google, an impeccably dressed, sports-
oriented husband who neglected his long-suffering wife, domi-
nated the strip, but when the *Chicago Herald* was sold to Hearst
in 1919, the strip, then retitled TAKE BARNEY GOOGLE, FOR
INSTANCE, began to evolve in new directions. Eventually,
Barney travelled south where, in 1934, he met the hillbilly
character Snuffy Smith, who eventually took over the strip. The
films adapted from the strip are negligible "B" picture fodder.

BARRY McKENZIE
newspaper strip

ADVENTURES OF BARRY McKENZIE (Longford, 1972)—
theatrical feature; 117 minutes; color.

Credits: Producer: Phillip Adams; Director: Bruce Beresford;
Screenplay: Bruce Beresford, Barry Humphries; Camera: Don

McAlpine; Music: Peter Best; Editor: John Scott; Costumes: June Hamilton.

Cast: Barry Crocker (Barry McKenzie); Barry Humphries (Edna Everage/Hoot/Himself); Paul Bertram (Curly); Dennis Price (Mr. Gort); Avice Landon (Mrs. Gort); Peter Cook (Dominic); Mary Anne Severne (Lesley); Dick Bentley (Detective); Spike Milligan (Landlord); Jonathan Hardy (Groove Courtenay); Julie Covington (Blanche); Jenny Tomasin (Sarah Gort); Chris Malcolm (Sean); Judith Furze (Claude); Maria O'Brien (Caroline Thighs); John Joyce (Maurie Miller); Margo Lloyd (Mrs. McKenzie).

BARRY McKENZIE HOLDS HIS OWN (Roadshow Release, 1975)—theatrical feature; 120 minutes; color.

Credits: Producer: Bruce Beresford; Director: Bruce Beresford; Screenplay: Barry Humphries, Bruce Beresford; Camera: Don McAlpine; Music: Peter Best; Editor: William Anderson; Production Design: John Stoddart.

Cast: Barry Crocker (Barry McKenzie/Ken McKenzie); Barry Humphries (Edna Everage/Senator Douglas Manton/Dr. Meyer de Lamphrey/Buck-toothed Englishman); Donald Pleasance (Count Plasma); Dick Bentley (Colonel Lucas); Ed Devereaux (Sir Alex Ferguson); Tommy Trinder (Arthur McKenzie); Roy Kinnear (Bishop of Parts); John Le Mesurier (English Emigrant); Beatrice Aston (Cherylene McKenzie); Katya Wyeth (Germaine); Marcelle Jordine (Rhonda Cutforth-Jones).

Created by writer Barry Humphries and artist Nicholas Garland in 1967, this British humor strip inspired two feature films. Strip creator Barry Humphries appeared in both movie adaptations of the "adult" comic strip, and the resulting films enjoyed a degree of success in Australia, but were poorly distributed elsewhere. The strip related the misadventures of a bumbling innocent abroad, with both films grasping desperately for laughs, the second picture even degenerating into failed horror-movie satire.

BATMAN
comic book
National Periodicals/DC Comics

BATMAN (Columbia, 1943)—theatrical serial; 15 chapters, first chapter approximately 30 minutes, remaining chapters approximately 20 minutes each.

BATMAN (Columbia, 1943): Lewis Wilson, Douglas Croft.

Credits: Producer: Rudolph C. Flothow; Director: Lambert Hillyer; Screenplay: Victor McLeod, Leslie Swabacker, Harry Fraser; Camera: James S. Brown, Jr.; Music: Lee Zahler; Editors: Dwight Caldwell, Earl Turner; Assistant Director: Gene Anderson.

Cast: Lewis Wilson (Batman/Bruce Wayne); Douglas Croft (Robin/Dick Grayson); J. Carrol Naish (Dr. Daka); Shirley Patterson (Linda); William Austin (Alfred); Charles C. Wilson (Captain Arnold); Charles Middleton (Ken Colton); Robert Fiske (Foster); Michael Vallon (Preston); Gus Glassmire (Martin Warren).

Chapter Titles: (1) The Electrical Brain; (2) The Bat's Cave; (3) The Mark of the Zombies; (4) Slaves of the Rising Sun; (5) The Living Corpse; (6) Poison Peril; (7) The Phoney Doctor; (8) Lured by Radium; (9) The Sign of the Sphinx; (10) Flying Spies; (11) A Nipponese Trap; (12) Embers of Evil; (13) Eight Steps Down; (14) The Executioner Strikes; (15) The Doom of the Rising Sun.

Note: This serial was reissued—in its fifteen-chapter entirety—as AN EVENING WITH BATMAN AND ROBIN in 1965.

BATMAN AND ROBIN (Columbia, 1949)—theatrical serial; 15 chapters, first chapter approximately 30 minutes, remaining chapters approximately 20 minutes each.

Credits: Producer: Sam Katzman; Director: Spencer G. Bennet; Screenplay: George H. Plympton, Joseph F. Poland, Royal K. Cole; Camera: Ira H. Morgan; Music: Mischa Bakaleinikoff; Editors: Earl Turner, Dwight Caldwell; Assistant Director: R. M. Andrews.

Cast: Robert Lowery (Batman/Bruce Wayne); John Duncan (Robin/Dick Grayson); Jane Adams (Vicki Vale); Lyle Talbot

(Commissioner Gordon); Ralph Graves (Harrison); Don C. Harvey (Nolan); William Fawcett (Professor Hammil); Leonard Penn (Carter); Rick Vallin (Barry Brown); Michael Whalen (Dunne); Greg McClure (Evans); House Peters, Jr. (Earl); Jim Diehl (Jason); Eric Wilson (Alfred); Marshall Bradford (Roger Morton).

Chapter Titles: (1) Batman Takes Over; (2) Tunnel of Terror; (3) Robin's Wild Ride; (4) Batman Trapped; (5) Robin Rescues Batman; (6) Target—Robin; (7) The Fatal Blast; (8) Robin Meets the Wizard; (9) The Wizard Strikes Back; (10) Batman's Last Chance; (11) Robin's Ruse; (12) Robin Rides the Wind; (13) The Wizard's Challenge; (14) Batman vs. the Wizard; (15) Batman Victorious.

BATMAN AND ROBIN (Columbia, 1949): John Duncan, Robert Lowery.

Note: This serial is sometimes referred to as THE NEW ADVENTURES OF BATMAN AND ROBIN, but the main title of the film itself is simply BATMAN AND ROBIN.

BATMAN (ABC, 1966–68)—TV series; 120 episodes, 30 minutes each; color.

Credits: Executive Producer: William Dozier; Producer: Howie Horwitz; Series Directors: Sam Strangis, Oscar Rudolph, Larry Preece, George Waggner, James Clark, James Sheldon, Robert Butler, Norman Foster, Tom Gries, William A. Graham, Leslie H. Martinson, Charles R. Rondeau, Richard Sarafian, Don Weis; Series Writers: Lorenzo Semple, Jr., Robert Dozier, Max Hodge,

BATMAN (ABC-TV, 1966): Burt Ward, Adam West.

Fred De Gorter, Charles Hoffman, Stephen Kandel, Stanley Ralph Ross, Lee Orgel, John Caldwell, Jack Paritz, Bob Rodgers, Francis Cockrell, Robert C. Dennis, Earl Barret, Rik Vollaerts, Dick Carr, Sheldon Stark; Camera: Sam Levitt, Howard Schwartz; Art Directors: Jack Martin Smith, Serge Krizman; Music: Nelson Riddle, Billy May; Music Supervision: Lionel Newman, Theme Music: Neil Hefti; Theme Music (Batgirl Theme): Billy May; Lyrics (Batgirl Theme): Willy Mack.

Cast: Adam West (Batman/Bruce Wayne); Burt Ward (Robin/ Dick Grayson); Yvonne Craig (Batgirl/Barbara Gordon); Alan Napier (Alfred); Neil Hamilton (Commissioner Gordon); Madge Blake (Aunt Harriet); Stafford Repp (Chief O'Hara); Burgess Meredith (The Penguin); Cesar Romero (The Joker); Frank Gorshin, John Astin (The Riddler); Julie Newmar, Eartha Kitt (The Catwoman); Art Carney (The Archer); Glynis Johns (Lady Penelope Peasoup); Rudy Vallee (Lord Marmaduke Ffogg); Roger C. Carmel (Colonel Gumm); Tallulah Bankhead (The Black Widow); Vincent Price (Egghead); Ann Baxter (Olga); Ida Lupino (Dr. Cassandra); Howard Duff (Cabala); Malachi Throne (Falseface); Michael Rennie (The Sandman); Maurice Evans (The Puzzler); Kathleen Crowley (Sophie Starr); Liberace (Chandell); David Wayne (The Mad Hatter); George Sanders, Eli Wallach, Otto Preminger (Mr. Freeze); Shelley Winters (Ma Parker); Walter Slezak (Clock King); Van Johnson (The Minstrel); Joan Collins (The Siren); Cliff Robertson (Shame); Carolyn Jones (Marsha, Queen of Diamonds); Milton Berle (Louie the Lilac); Roddy McDowall (The Bookworm); John Crawford (The Devil); Victor Buono (King Tut); Zsa Zsa Gabor (Minerva); Barbara Rush (Nora Clavicle); Byron Keith (Mayor John Lindseed); Jean Byron (Millie Lindseed); Ethel Merman (Lola Lasagne); William Dozier (Narrator).

BATMAN (Twentieth Century-Fox, 1966)—theatrical feature; 105 minutes; color.

Credits: Producer: William Dozier; Director: Leslie H. Martinson; Screenplay: Lorenzo Semple, Jr.; Camera: Howard Schwartz; Music: Nelson Riddle; "Batman Theme": Neal Hefti; Editor: Harry Gerstad.

Cast: Adam West (Batman/Bruce Wayne); Burt Ward (Robin/Dick Grayson); Lee Meriwether (The Catwoman/Miss Kitka); Burgess Meredith (The Penguin); Frank Gorshin (The Riddler); Cesar Romero (The Joker); Alan Napier (Alfred); Neil Hamilton (Commissioner Gordon); Stafford Repp (Chief O'Hara); Madge Blake (Aunt Harriet); Reginald Denny (Commodore Schmidlapp); Milton Frome (Vice-Admiral Fangschliester); Gil Perkins (Bluebeard); Dick Crockett (Morgan); George Sawaya (Quetch).

BATMAN (Warner Bros., 1989)—theatrical feature; 126 minutes; color.

Credits: Producers: Jon Peters, Peter Guber; Co-Producer: Chris Kenny; Executive Producers: Benjamin Milniker, Michael Uslan; Director: Tim Burton; Screenplay: Sam Hamm, Warren Skarren; Camera: Roger Pratt; Editor: Ray Lovejoy; Costumes: Bob Ringwood; Production Design: Anton Furst; Art Directors: Terry Ackland-Snow, Nigel Phelps; Assistant Director: Derek Crackwell; Supervising Production Accountant: Mike Smith; Supervising Art Director: Les Tomkins; Set Decorator: Peter Young; Storyboard Artist: Michael White; Props: Charles Torbett; Casting: Marion Dougherty; Camera Operators: Mike Proudfoot; John Campbell; Script Supervisor: Cheryl Leigh; Sound: Tony Dawe; Supervising Sound Editor: Don Sharpe; Makeup: Paul Engelen; Prosthetic Makeup: Nick Dudman; Hair Dresser: Colin Jamison; Special Effects: Derek Meddings; Miniature Photography: John Evans; Construction Manager: Terry Apsey; Second Unit Direction/Photography: Peter McDonald; Assistant Director: Steven Harding; Camera Operator: Mike Brewster; Sound: David Allen; Chief Electrician: Bob Bremner.

Cast: Jack Nicholson (Jack Napier/The Joker); Michael Keaton (Batman/Bruce Wayne); Kim Basinger (Vicki Vale); Jack Palance (Carl Grissom); Robert Wuhl (Alexander Knox); Billy Dee Williams (Harvey Dent); Pat Hingle (Commissioner Gordon); Jerry Hall (Alicia); Michael Gough (Alfred); Lee Wallage (Mayor Borg); Tracy Walter (Bob the Goon); William Hootkins (Eckhardt); Edwin Craig (Rotelli); John Dair (Ricorso); Steve Plytas (Doctor); Richard Strange, Carl Chase, Mac MacDonald, George Cooper, Phil Tan, Terence Plummer (Goons); Hugo E. Blick (Young Jack Napier); Charles Roskilly (Young Bruce Wayne); George Roth (Eddie); Christopher Fairbank (Nick); David Baxt (Mr. Wayne); Sharon Holm (Mrs. Wayne).

Created by artist Bob Kane and writer Bill Finger, Batman made his print debut in DETECTIVE COMICS #27 in May of 1939. Kane's costumed hero combined such seemingly disparate elements as the heroism of Douglas Fairbanks' character in THE MARK OF ZORRO (1920) and the dark mystery of the film THE BAT WHISPERS (1930), directed by Roland West. Kane has admitted that both of these films, as well as the Conrad Veidt character in THE MAN WHO LAUGHS (1927), whose facial deformity inspired the creation of Batman's foe The Joker, were deeply influential in the creation of one of the most popular and successful characters in the comic book industry.

Of the two serial adaptations produced by Columbia Pictures, the 1943 version starring Lewis Wilson is by far the better effort, with some nice atmospheric touches (the scenes of Batman interrogating criminals in his Bat's Cave are particularly melodramatic) and (by serial standards at least) decent production values. J. Carrol Naish, a far better actor than was usually found in serials, portrayed the nefarious Dr. Daka, a crazed Japanese spy intent on stealing Gotham City's radium supply in order to aid the Axis cause. Daka and his army of gangsters and laboratory-created zombies are, of course, defeated at every turn by Batman and Robin. This serial was directed by Lambert Hillyer, an experienced hand at "B" westerns whose two other forays into the realm of fantasy/horror were also notable: DRACULA'S DAUGHTER (1936) and THE INVISIBLE RAY (1936). There are many scenes in BATMAN that linger in the memory; the film has a nice texture and (to its credit) looks a bit older than it is, which helps a bit in the atmosphere department. The main flaw is in the plot construction. Although the Dr. Daka character is well aware of Batman, and attempts to destroy him from the beginning of the serial, Batman (aside from briefly mentioning his opponent in Chapter 1) seems unaware of who the mastermind is, and does not even confront Daka until the final episode.

The later 1949 follow-up, BATMAN AND ROBIN, starring Robert Lowery as Batman, is abominable. One of producer Sam Katzman's most impoverished efforts (the first serial had been produced by Rudolph C. Flothow), BATMAN AND ROBIN is badly crippled by an incredibly low budget, limp direction (the camera is often totally static, seemingly nailed to the floor), and indifferent acting. Robert Lowery is nearly catatonic as Batman, and John Duncan, far too mature for the role of Robin (Duncan actually looks *older* than Lowery in some scenes), is equally ineffective.

The less said about the Adam West TV series of the 1960s, the better. Despite its overwhelming popularity, the show generally derided its source, and was almost singlehandedly responsible for popularizing the dubious concept of intentional "camp" (which one critic has aptly described as "the lowest form of artistic expression known to man"), a disparaging point of view that has seriously impaired many subsequent films derived from similar material, such as DOC SAVAGE, THE MAN OF BRONZE (1975), and FLASH GORDON (1980). Nevertheless, the casting of the villains in the TV series was often effective, particularly Frank Gorshin as The Riddler and Julie Newmar as The Catwoman, but Adam West's physique, as well as his performance, left a lot to be desired as Batman, and Burt Ward was insufferable as Robin.

The 1989 feature starring Michael Keaton as Batman was

lavishly produced, darkly ominous in mood and heavily (perhaps *too* heavily) atmospheric, but it was a welcome return to a serious approach, and wisely ignored the previous TV series. The physically slight Keaton, cast solely for his current box-office value, does much better than one would expect in the title role, but Jack Nicholson dominates the film with his maniacal performance as The Joker, with Kim Basinger lending nice support as reporter Vicki Vale, a character that Kane claims was inspired by the young Marilyn Monroe, whom he met in Hollywood when he was serving as a consultant during production of the Robert Lowery serial. Although somewhat flawed by its overly elaborate production design and unnecessary psychological pretensions, BATMAN is generally effective and is at least far superior to the disappointing Christopher Reeve SUPERMAN movies.

BLACKHAWK
comic book
Quality Comics/National Periodicals/DC Comics

BLACKHAWK (Columbia, 1952)—theatrical serial; 15 chapters, first chapter approximately 30 minutes, remaining chapters approximately 20 minutes each.

Credits: Producer: Sam Katzman; Directors: Spencer G. Bennet, Fred F. Sears; Screenplay: George H. Plympton, Royal K. Cole, Sherman L. Lowe; Camera: William Whitley; Music: Mischa Bakaleinikoff; Editor: Earl Turner; Assistant Director: Charles B. Gould.

Cast: Kirk Alyn (Blackhawk); Carol Forman (Laska); John Crawford (Chuck); Michael Fox (William Case); Don C. Harvey (Olaf); Rick Vallin (Stan/Boris); Larry Stewart (André); Weaver Levy (Chop Chop); Zon Murray (Bork); Nick Stuart (Cress); Marshall Reed (Aller); Pierce Lyden (Dyke); William

BLACKHAWK (Columbia, 1952): Kirk Alyn takes a hard right to the chin.

Fawcett (Dr. Rolph); Rory Mallinson (Hodge); Frank Ellis (Hendrickson).

Chapter Titles: (1) Distress Call from Space; (2) Blackhawk Traps a Traitor; (3) In the Enemy's Hideout; (4) The Iron Monster; (5) Human Targets; (6) Blackhawk's Leap for Life; (7) Mystery Fuel; (8) Blasted from the Sky; (9) Blackhawk Tempts Fate; (10) Chase for Element X; (11) Forced Down; (12) Drums of Doom; (13) Blackhawk's Daring Plan; (14) Blackhawk's Wild Ride; (15) The Leader Unmasked.

Created for MILITARY COMICS #1 in August of 1941, BLACKHAWK was a violent war strip pitting a band of intrepid adventurers against the Axis forces. The Columbia Pictures serial based on the strip was an inevitably cheap Sam Katzman production suffering from miscasting and a lack of scope. Lead

Kirk Alyn does well enough as Blackhawk, though, and Carol Forman, who appeared with Alyn in Katzman's hugely successful SUPERMAN serial, is memorable as an evil spy.

BLONDIE
newspaper strip

BLONDIE (Columbia, 1938)—theatrical feature; 68 minutes.

Credits: Producer: Robert Sparks; Director: Frank R. Strayer; Screenplay: Richard Flournoy; Camera: Henry Freulich; Editor: Gene Havlick.

Cast: Penny Singleton (Blondie); Arthur Lake (Dagwood); Larry Simms (Baby Dumpling); Gene Lockhart (C. P. Hazlip); Ann Doran (Elsie Hazlip); Jonathan Hale (J. C. Dithers); Gordon Oliver (Chester Franey); Stanley Andrews (Mr. Hicks); Danny Mummert (Alvin Fuddle); Kathleen Lockhart (Mrs. Miller); Dorothy Moore (Dorothy); Fay Helm (Mrs. Fuddle); Richard Fiske (Nelson); Daisy (Himself); Irving Bacon (Mailman); Ian Wolfe (Judge).

BLONDIE BRINGS UP BABY (Columbia, 1939)—theatrical feature; 67 minutes.

Credits: Producer: Robert Sparks; Director: Frank R. Strayer; Screenplay: Gladys Lehman, Richard Flournoy (Original Story: Robert Chapin, Karen De Wolf, Richard Flournoy); Camera: Henry Freulich; Music: Morris Stoloff; Editor: Otto Meyer; Art Director: Lionel Banks.

Cast: Penny Singleton (Blondie); Arthur Lake (Dagwood); Larry Simms (Baby Dumpling); Danny Mummert (Alvin Fuddle); Jonathan Hale (J. C. Dithers); Robert Middlemass

(Abner Cartwright); Olin Howland (Book Agent); Fay Helm (Mrs. Fuddle); Peggy Ann Garner (Melinda Mason); Roy Gordon (Mason); Grace Stafford (Miss White); Helen Jerome Eddy (School Principal); Irving Bacon (Mailman); Robert Sterling (Salesman); Bruce Bennett (Chauffeur); Ian Wolfe (Police Judge); Daisy (Himself).

BLONDIE MEETS THE BOSS (Columbia, 1939)— theatrical feature; 75 minutes.

Credits: Producer: Robert Sparks; Director: Frank R. Strayer; Screenplay: Richard Flournoy (Original Story: Kay Van Riper, Richard Flournoy); Camera: Henry Freulich; Editor: Gene Havlick.

Cast: Penny Singleton (Blondie); Arthur Lake (Dagwood); Larry Simms (Baby Dumpling); Dorothy Moore (Dot); Jonathan Hale (J. C. Dithers); Don Beddoe (Marvin); Linda Winters (Francine); Danny Mummert (Alvin Fuddle); Stanley Brown (Ollie); Joel Dean (Freddie); Richard Fiske (Nelson); Inez Courtney (Betty Lou); Irving Bacon (Mailman); James Craig; Robert Sterling.

BLONDIE TAKES A VACATION (Columbia, 1939)— theatrical feature; 68 minutes.

Credits: Producer: Robert Sparks; Director: Frank R. Strayer; Screenplay: Richard Flournoy (Original Story: Karen De Wolf, Robert Chapin, Richard Flournoy); Camera: Henry Freulich; Editor: Viola Lawrence.

Cast: Penny Singleton (Blondie); Arthur Lake (Dagwood); Larry Simms (Baby Dumpling); Danny Mummert (Alvin Fuddle); Donald Meek (Jonathan Gillis); Donald MacBride (Harvey Morton); Thomas W. Ross (Matthew Dickerson); Elizabeth Dunne (Mrs. Dickerson); Robert Wilcox (John

Larkin); Harlan Briggs (Holden); Irving Bacon (Mailman); Milt Kibbee (Creditor); Daisy (Himself).

BLONDIE HAS SERVANT TROUBLE (Columbia, 1940)—theatrical feature; 69 minutes.

Credits: Producer: Robert Sparks; Director: Frank R. Strayer; Screenplay: Richard Flournoy (Original Story: Albert Duffy); Camera: Henry Freulich; Music: Leigh Harline; Editor: Gene Havlick.

Cast: Penny Singleton (Blondie); Arthur Lake (Dagwood); Larry Simms (Baby Dumpling); Danny Mummert (Alvin Fuddle); Jonathan Hale (J. C. Dithers); Arthur Hohl (Eric Vaughn); Esther Dale (Anna Vaughn); Irving Bacon (Mailman); Ray Turner (Horatio Jones); Walter Soldering (Morgan); Fay Helm (Mrs. Fuddle); Murray Alper (Taxi Driver); Eddie Laughton (Photographer); Daisy (Himself).

BLONDIE ON A BUDGET (Columbia, 1940)—theatrical feature; 72 minutes.

Credits: Producer: Robert Sparks; Director: Frank R. Strayer; Screenplay: Richard Flournoy (Original Story: Charles Molyneaux Brown); Camera: Henry Freulich; Editor: Gene Havlick; Music: Morris Stoloff; Art Director: Lionel Banks; Costumes: Ray Howell.

Cast: Penny Singleton (Blondie); Arthur Lake (Dagwood); Larry Simms (Baby Dumpling); Rita Hayworth (Joan Forrester); Danny Mummert (Alvin Fuddle); Don Beddoe (Marvin Williams); John Qualen (Mr. Fuddle); Fay Helm (Mrs. Fuddle); Irving Bacon (Mailman); Thurston Hall (Brice); William Brisbane (Theater Manager); Emory Parnell (Dempsey); Willie Best (Black Boy); Hal K. Dawson (Bank Teller); Chester Clute (Ticket Agent); Dick Curtis (Mechanic); George Guhl (Platt); Janet Shaw, Claire James (Usherettes); Mary Currier, Rita

Owin (Salesladies); Gene Morgan (Man); Jack Egan (Elevator Man); Ralph Peters (Bartender); Daisy (Himself).

BLONDIE PLAYS CUPID (Columbia, 1940)—theatrical feature; 67 minutes.

Credits: Producer: Robert Sparks; Director: Frank R. Strayer; Screenplay: Richard Flournoy, Karen De Wolf (Original Story:

BLONDIE PLAYS CUPID (Columbia, 1940): Penny Singleton as Blondie.

Charles M. Brown, Karen De Wolf); Camera: Henry Freulich; Editor: Gene Milford.

Cast: Penny Singleton (Blondie); Arthur Lake (Dagwood); Larry Simms (Baby Dumpling); Ruth Terry (Lovey Nelson); Tito Guizar (Don Rodriguez); Jonathan Hale (J. C. Dithers); Danny Mummert (Alvin Fuddle); Irving Bacon (Mailman); Glenn Ford (Charlie); Luana Walters (Millie); Will Wright (Tucker); Spencer Charters (Uncle Abner); Leona Roberts (Aunt Hannah); Tommy Dixon (Saunders); Rex Moore (Newsboy); Daisy (Himself).

BLONDIE GOES LATIN (Columbia, 1941)—theatrical feature; 70 minutes (*GB:* CONGA SWING).

Credits: Producer: Robert Sparks; Director: Frank R. Strayer; Screenplay: Richard Flournoy, Karen De Wolf (Original Story: Quinn Martin); Camera: Henry Freulich; Music: Morris Stoloff; Editor: Gene Havlick; Music and Lyrics: Chet Forrest, Bob Wright.

Cast: Penny Singleton (Blondie); Arthur Lake (Dagwood); Larry Simms (Baby Dumpling); Ruth Terry (Lovey Nelson); Tito Guizar (Don Rodriguez); Jonathan Hale (J. C. Dithers); Danny Mummert (Alvin Fuddle); Irving Bacon (Mailman); Janet Burston (Little Girl); Kirby Grant (Hal Trent); Joseph King (Captain); Eddie Acuff (Cab Driver); Harry Barris (Musician); Daisy (Himself).

BLONDIE IN SOCIETY (Columbia, 1941)—theatrical feature; 77 minutes (*GB:* HENPECKED).

Credits: Producer: Robert Sparks; Director: Frank R. Strayer; Screenplay: Karen De Wolf (Original Story: Eleanore Griffin); Camera: Henry Freulich; Editor: Charles Nelson; Music: M. W. Stoloff; Art Director: Lionel Banks.

Cast: Penny Singleton (Blondie); Arthur Lake (Dagwood); Larry Simms (Baby Dumpling); Jonathan Hale (J. C. Dithers); Danny Mummert (Alvin Fuddle); William Frawley (Waldo Pincus); Edgar Kennedy (Doctor); Chick Chandler (Cliff Peters); Irving Bacon (Mailman); Bill Goodwin (Announcer); Gary Owen (Carpenter); Tommy Dixon (Saunders); Robert Mitchell's Boys Choir; Daisy (Himself).

BLONDIE FOR VICTORY (Columbia, 1942)—theatrical feature; 72 minutes (*GB:* TROUBLES THROUGH BULLETS).

Credits: Producer: Robert Sparks; Director: Frank R. Strayer; Screenplay: Karen De Wolf, Connie Lee (Original Story: Fay Kanin); Camera: Henry Freulich; Editor: Al Clark.

Cast: Penny Singleton (Blondie); Arthur Lake (Dagwood); Larry Simms (Baby Dumpling); Marjorie White (Cookie); Stuart Erwin (Herschel Smith); Jonathan Hale (J. C. Dithers); Danny Mummert (Alvin Fuddle); Danny Gargan (Sergeant); Renie Riano (Mrs. Clabber); Irving Bacon (Mr. Crumb); Harrison Green (Mr. Green); Charles Wagenheim (Hoarder); Sylvia Field (Mrs. Williams); Georgia Backus (Mrs. Jones); Daisy (Himself).

BLONDIE GOES TO COLLEGE (Columbia, 1942)— theatrical feature; 74 minutes (*GB:* THE BOSS SAID NO).

Credits: Producer: Robert Sparks; Director: Frank R. Strayer; Screenplay: Lou Breslow (Original Story: Warren Wilson, Clyde Bruckman); Camera: Henry Freulich; Music: M. W. Stoloff; Editor: Otto Meyer.

Cast: Penny Singleton (Blondie); Arthur Lake (Dagwood); Larry Simms (Baby Dumpling); Janet Blair (Laura Wadsworth); Jonathan Hale (J. C. Dithers); Danny Mummert (Alvin Fuddle); Larry Parks (Rusty Bryant); Adele Mara (Babs

BLONDIE FOR VICTORY (Columbia, 1942): Arthur Lake (swathed in bandages) and Penny Singleton.

Connelly); Lloyd Bridges (Ben Dixon); Sidney Melton (Mouse Gifford); Andrew Tombes (J. J. Wadsworth); Esther Dale (Mrs. Dill); Bill Goodwin (Announcer); Daisy (Himself).

BLONDIE'S BLESSED EVENT (Columbia, 1942)— theatrical feature; 69 minutes.

Credits: Producer: Robert Sparks; Director: Frank R. Strayer; Screenplay: Connie Lee, Karen De Wolf, Richard Flournoy; Camera: Henry Freulich; Editor: Charles Nelson.

Cast: Penny Singleton (Blondie); Arthur Lake (Dagwood); Larry Simms (Baby Dumpling); Norma Jean Wayne (Cookie); Jonathan Hale (J. C. Dithers); Danny Mummert (Alvin Fuddle); Hans Conreid (George Wickley); Stanley Brown (Ollie); Irving Bacon (Mr. Crumb); Mary Wickes (Sarah Miller); Paul Harvey

(William Lawrence); Dorothy Ann Seese (Little Girl); Arthur O'Connell (Intern); Don Barclay (Waiter); Daisy (Himself).

FOOTLIGHT GLAMOUR (Columbia, 1943)—theatrical feature; 68 minutes.

Credits: Producer and Director: Frank R. Strayer; Screenplay: Connie Lee, Karen De Wolf; Camera: Philip Tannura; Editor: Richard Fantl; Music: M. W. Stoloff; Art Director: Lionel Banks; Music and Lyrics (for the songs "What's Under Your Mask, Madame?" and "Bamboola"): Ray Evans, Jay Livingston.

Cast: Penny Singleton (Blondie); Arthur Lake (Dagwood); Larry Simms (Alexander); Ann Savage (Vicki Wheeler); Jonathan Hale (J. C. Dithers); Irving Bacon (Mr. Crumb); Marjorie Ann Mutchie (Cookie); Danny Mummert (Alvin Fuddle); Thurston Hall (Randolph Wheeler); Grace Hale (Mrs. Dithers); Rafael Storm (Jerry Grant); Arthur Loft (Mr. Clark); James Flavin (Father); Daisy (Himself).

IT'S A GREAT LIFE (Columbia, 1943)—theatrical feature; 68 minutes.

Credits: Producer and Director: Frank R. Strayer. Screenplay: Connie Lee, Karen De Wolf; Camera: L. W. O'Connell; Music: M. W. Stoloff; Editor: Al Clark; Art Director: Lionel Banks.

Cast: Penny Singleton (Blondie); Arthur Lake (Dagwood); Larry Simms (Alexander); Hugh Herbert (Timothy Brewster); Jonathan Hale (J. C. Dithers); Danny Mummert (Alvin Fuddle); Alan Dineheart (Collender Martin); Douglas Leavitt (Bromley); Irving Bacon (Mailman); Marjorie Ann Mutchie (Cookie): Si Jenks (Piano Tuner): Ray Walker (Salesman); Dickie Dillon (Bit Boy); Daisy (Himself); Reggie (the Horse).

LEAVE IT TO BLONDIE (Columbia, 1945)—theatrical feature; 74 minutes.

Credits: Producer: Burt Kelly; Director: Abby Berlin; Screenplay: Connie Lee; Camera: Franz F. Planer; Editor: Al Clark; Art Direction: Perry Smith.

Cast: Penny Singleton (Blondie); Arthur Lake (Dagwood); Larry Simms (Alexander); Marjorie Weaver (Rita Rogers); Jonathan Hale (Mr. Dithers); Chick Chandler (Eddie Baxter); Danny Mummert (Alvin Fuddle); Marjorie Ann Mutchie (Cookie); Eula Morgan (Mrs. Meredith); Arthur Space (Mr. Fuddle); Eddie Acuff (Mailman); Fred Graff (Henry); Jack Rice (Ollie); Maude Eberne (Magda); Ann Loos (Mary); Manlyn Johnson (Secretary); Daisy (Himself).

BLONDIE KNOWS BEST (Columbia, 1946)—theatrical feature; 69 minutes.

Credits: Producer: Burt Kelly; Director: Abby Berlin; Screenplay: Edward Bernds, Al Martin (Original Story: Edward Bernds); Camera: Phillip Tannura; Music: Mischa Bakaleinikoff; Editor: Aaron Stell.

Cast: Penny Singleton (Blondie); Arthur Lake (Dagwood); Larry Simms (Baby Dumpling); Marjorie Kent (Cookie); Steven Geary (Dr. Schmidt); Jonathan Hale (J. C. Dithers); Shemp Howard (Jim Gray); Jerome Cowan (Charles Peabody); Danny Mummert (Alvin Fuddle); Ludwig Donath (Dr. Titus); Arthur Loft (Conroy); Edwin Cooper (David Armstrong); Jack Rice (Ollie); Alyn Lockwood (Mary); Carol Hughes (Gloria Evans); Kay Mallory (Ruth Evans).

BLONDIE'S LUCKY DAY (Columbia, 1946)—theatrical feature; 69 minutes.

Credits: Producer: Burt Kelly; Director: Abby Berlin; Screenplay: Connie Lee; Camera: L. W. O'Connell; Editor: Aaron Stell; Music: Mischa Bakaleinikoff.

Cast: Penny Singleton (Blondie); Arthur Lake (Dagwood); Larry Simms (Alexander); Marjorie Kent (Cookie); Robert Stanton (Johnny); Angelyn Orr (Mary Jane); Jonathan Hale (J. C. Dithers); Paul Harvey (Mr. Butler); Bobby Larson (Tommy); Jack Rice (Ollie); Charles Arnt (Mayor); Margie Liszt (Mary); Frank Orth (Salesman); Frank Jenks (Postman); Daisy (Himself).

LIFE WITH BLONDIE (Columbia, 1946)—theatrical feature; 69 minutes.

Credits: Producer: Burt Kelly; Director: Abby Berlin; Screenplay: Connie Lee; Camera: L. W. O'Connell; Editor: Jerome Thomas; Music: Mischa Bakaleinikoff.

Cast: Penny Singleton (Blondie); Arthur Lake (Dagwood); Larry Simms (Alexander); Marjorie Kent (Cookie); Jonathan Hale (Mr. Dithers); Ernest Truex (Glassby); Marc Lawrence (Pete); Veda Ann Borg (Hazel); Jack Rice (Ollie); Bobby Larson (Tommy); Doug Fowley (Blackie); George Tyne (Cassidy); Edward Gargan (Dogcatcher); Francis Pierlot (Rutledge); Ray Walker (Anthony); Eddie Acuff (Mailman); Robert Ryan (Second Policeman); Steve Benton (Driver); Daisy (Himself).

BLONDIE IN THE DOUGH (Columbia, 1947)—theatrical feature; 69 minutes.

Credits: Director: Abby Berlin; Screenplay: Arthur Marx, Jack Henley (Original Story: Jack Marx); Camera: Vincent Farrar; Music: Mischa Bakaleinikoff; Editor: Henry Batista.

LIFE WITH BLONDIE (Columbia, 1946): Arthur Lake as Dagwood and Jonathan Hale as Mr. Dithers.

Cast: Penny Singleton (Blondie); Arthur Lake (Dagwood); Larry Simms (Alexander); Marjorie Kent (Cookie); Jerome Cowan (Radcliffe); Hugh Herbert (Llewellyn Simmons); Clarence Kolb (J. T. Thorpe); Danny Mummert (Alvin Fuddle); Eddie Acuff (Mailman); Norman Phillips (Ollie); Kernan Cripps (Baxter); Fred Sears (Quinn); Boyd Davis (First Board Member); Mary Emery (Mrs. Thorpe); Daisy (Himself).

BLONDIE'S ANNIVERSARY (Columbia, 1947)—theatrical feature; 67 minutes.

Credits: Director: Abby Berlin; Screenplay: Jack Henley; Camera: Vincent Farrar; Music: Mischa Bakaleinikoff; Editor: Al Clark; Art Director: George Brooks.

Cast: Penny Singleton (Blondie); Arthur Lake (Dagwood); Larry Simms (Alexander); Marjorie Kent (Cookie); Grant Mitchell (Samuel Breckinridge); William Frawley (Sharkey); Edmund McDonald (Burley); Fred Sears (Dalton); Jack Rice (Ollie); Alyn Lockwood (Mary); Frank Wilcox (Carter); Eddie Acuff (Mailman); Larry Steers (Parker); Al Zeidman.

BLONDIE'S BIG MOMENT (Columbia, 1947)—theatrical feature; 69 minutes (*GB:* BUNDLE OF TROUBLE).

Credits: Producer: Burt Kelly; Director: Abby Berlin; Screenplay: Connie Lee; Camera: Allen Siegler; Editor: Jerome Thomas; Music: Mischa Bakaleinikoff; Art Director: George Brooks.

Cast: Penny Singleton (Blondie); Arthur Lake (Dagwood); Larry Simms (Alexander); Marjorie Kent (Cookie); Anita Louise (Mrs. Gray); Jerome Cowan (Radcliffe); Danny Mummert (Alvin Fuddle); Jack Rice (Ollie); Jack Davis (Mr. Greenleaf); Johnny Granath (Slugger); Hal K. Dawson (Mr. Little); Eddie Acuff (Mailman); Alyn Lockwood (Mary); Robert De Haven (Pete); Robert Stevens (Joe); Douglas Wood (Theodore Payson); Dick Wessel (Bus Driver); Daisy (Himself).

BLONDIE'S HOLIDAY (Columbia, 1947)—theatrical feature; 61 minutes.

Credits: Producer: Burt Kelly; Director: Abby Berlin; Screenplay: Connie Lee; Camera: Vincent Farrar; Editor: Jerome Thomas; Music: Carter DeHaven, Jr.

Cast: Penny Singleton (Blondie); Arthur Lake (Dagwood); Larry Simms (Alexander); Marjorie Kent (Cookie); Jerome Cowan (Radcliffe); Grant Mitchell (Samuel Breckinridge); Sid Tomack (Pete Brody); Mary Young (Mrs. Breckinridge); Jeff York (Paul Madison); Bobby Larson (Alvin Fuddle); Jody Gilbert (Cynthia Thompson); Jack Rice (Ollie); Alyn Lockwood (Mary); Eddie Acuff (Postman); Tim Ryan (Mike); Anne Nagel (Bea Mason); Rodney Bell (Tom Henley).

BLONDIE'S REWARD (Columbia, 1948)—theatrical feature; 65 minutes.

Credits: Director: Abby Berlin; Screenplay: Edward Bernds; Camera: Vincent Farrar; Editor: Al Clark; Music: Mischa Bakaleinikoff.

Cast: Penny Singleton (Blondie); Arthur Lake (Dagwood); Larry Simms (Alexander); Marjorie Kent (Cookie); Jerome Cowan (Radcliffe); Gay Nelson (Alice Dickson); Ross Ford (Ted Scott); Danny Mummert (Alvin Fuddle); Paul Harvey (John Dixon); Frank Jenks (Ed Vance); Chick Chandler (Bill Cooper); Jack Rice (Ollie); Eddie Acuff (Postman); Alyn Lockwood (Mary); Frank Sully (Officer Carney); Myron Healy (Cluett Day); Chester Clute (Leroy Blodgett).

BLONDIE'S SECRET (Columbia, 1948)—theatrical feature; 68 minutes.

Credits: Director: Edward Bernds; Screenplay: Jack Henley; Camera: Vincent Farrar; Editor: Al Clark; Music: Mischa Bakaleinikoff; Art Director: George Brooks.

Cast: Penny Singleton (Blondie); Arthur Lake (Dagwood); Larry Simms (Alexander); Marjorie Kent (Cookie); Jerome Cowan (Radcliffe); Thurston Hall (George Whiteside); Jack Rice (Ollie); Danny Mummert (Alvin Fuddle); Frank Orth (Dog Pound Attendant); Alyn Lockwood (Mary); Eddie Acuff (Mailman); Murray Alper (Larry); William "Bill" Phillips (Chips); Greta Granstedt (Mona); Grandon Rhodes (Ken Marcy); Paula Raymond (Nurse); Allen Matthews (Big Man); Joseph Crehan (Sergeant); Daisy (Himself).

BLONDIE HITS THE JACKPOT (Columbia, 1949)—theatrical feature; 66 minutes (*GB:* HITTING THE JACKPOT).

Credits: Producer: Ted Richmond; Director: Edward Bernds; Screenplay: Jack Henley; Camera: Vincent Farrar; Music: Mischa Bakaleinikoff; Editor: Henry Batista.

Cast: Penny Singleton (Blondie); Arthur Lake (Dagwood); Larry Simms (Alexander); Marjorie Kent (Cookie); Jerome Cowan (Radcliffe); Lloyd Corrigan (J. B. Hutchins); Danny Mummert (Alvin Fuddle); James Flavin (Brophy); Dick Wessel (Mailman); Ray Teal (Gus); Alyn Lockwood (Mary); Daisy (Himself).

BLONDIE'S BIG DEAL (Columbia, 1949)—theatrical feature; 66 minutes.

Credits: Producer: Ted Richmond; Director: Edward Bernds; Screenplay: Lucile Watson Henley; Camera: Vincent Farrar; Editor: Henry Batista.

Cast: Penny Singleton (Blondie); Arthur Lake (Dagwood); Larry Simms (Alexander); Marjorie Kent (Cookie); Jerome Cowan (Radcliffe); Collette Lyons (Norma); Wilton Graff (Dillon); Ray Walker (Stack); Stanley Andrews (Forsythe);

Alan Dineheart III (Rollo); Eddie Acuff (Mailman); Jack Rice (Ollie); Chester Clute (Mayor); George Lloyd (Fire Chief); Alyn Lockwood (Mary); Danny Mummert (Alvin Fuddle).

BEWARE OF BLONDIE (Columbia, 1950)—theatrical feature; 64 minutes.

Credits: Producer: Milton Feldman; Director: Edward Bernds; Screenplay: Jack Henley; Camera: Henry Freulich, Vincent Farrar; Editor: Richard Fantl.

Cast: Penny Singleton (Blondie); Arthur Lake (Dagwood); Larry Simms (Alexander); Marjorie Kent (Cookie); Adele Jergens (Toby Clifton); Dick Wessel (Mailman); Jack Rice (Ollie); Alyn Lockwood (Mary); Emory Parnell (Herb Woodley); Isabel Withers (Harriet Woodley); Danny Mummert (Alvin Fuddle); Douglas Fowley (Adolph); William E. Green (Samuel P. Dutton).

BLONDIE'S HERO (Columbia, 1950)—theatrical feature; 67 minutes.

Credits: Producer: Ted Richmond; Director: Edward Bernds; Screenplay: Jack Henley; Camera: Vincent Farrar; Editor: Henry Batista; Music: Mischa Bakaleinikoff; Art Director: Perry Smith.

Cast: Penny Singleton (Blondie); Arthur Lake (Dagwood); Larry Simms (Alexander); Marjorie Kent (Cookie); William Frawley (Marty Greer); Danny Mummert (Alvin Fuddle); Joe Sawyer (Sergeant Gateson); Teddy Infuhr (Danny Gateson); Alyn Lockwood (Mary Reynolds); Iris Adrian (Mae); Frank Jenks (Tim Saunders); Dick Wessel (Mailman); Jimmy Lloyd (Cpl. Biff Touhey); Robert Emmett Keane (J. Collins); Edward Earle (Richard Rogers); Mary Newton (Mrs. Rogers); Pat

Flaherty (Recruiting Sergeant); Ted Mapes (Fruit Salesman); Frank Wilcox (Captain Masters); Frank Sully (Mike McClusky); Daisy (Himself).

BLONDIE (NBC, 1957)—TV series; each episode 30 minutes.

Credits: Executive Producer: Hal Roach, Jr.; Producer: William Harmon; Associate Producer: John L. Greene; Series Directors: Hal Yates, Leslie Goodwins, Paul Landers; Series Writers: John L. Greene, Warren Spector, Gordon Hughes, Dick Mack, Harry Kronman; Camera: Paul Ivano, Paul Whitman; Art Direction: McClure Capps; Music: Leon Klatzkin; Animal Trainer: Rennie Renfro.

Cast: Pamela Britton (Blondie); Arthur Lake (Dagwood); Ann Barnes (Cookie); Stuffy Singer (Alexander); Florenz Ames (J. C. Dithers); Lela Bliss; Elvia Allman (Cora Dithers); Hal Peary (Herb Woodley); Lois Collier, Hollis Irving (Harriet Woodley); Pamela Duncan (Eloise); Lucien Littlefield (Mr. Beasley); Hazel Sherman (Louise Cooper); George Winslow (Foghorn).

BLONDIE (CBS, 1968–69)—TV series; each episode 30 minutes; color.

Credits: Executive Producer: Al Brodax; Producer: Joe Connelly; Associate Producer: Irving Paley; Director: Norman Abbott; Music: Bernard Green; Theme Music: Bernard Green (Lyrics: Al Brodax); Theme Vocal: Patricia Harty, Will Hutchins.

Cast: Patricia Harty (Blondie); Will Hutchins (Dagwood); Peter Robbins (Alexander); Pamelyn Ferdin (Cookie); Jim Backus (J. C. Dithers); Henny Backus (Cora Dithers); Bobbi Jordan (Tootsie Woodley); Marj Dusay (Gloria); Bryan O'Bryne (Mr. Beasley).

This famous humor strip was created by Chic Young for King Features Syndicate, the first installment appearing in September of 1930.

Young's popular strip about a bumbling young architect and his scatterbrained wife provided the basis for one of the longest running "B" movie comedy series in movie history. From 1938 to 1950, Columbia Pictures filmed twenty-eight BLONDIE features starring Penny Singleton as Blondie and Arthur Lake as Dagwood. In addition to comedy, this series offered generally tight plots and, at times, genuine emotional warmth. Singleton and Lake, talented performers, worked quite well together, and Singleton in particular contributed a great deal of charm to the films.

Originally, actress Shirley Deane had been cast as Blondie, but was replaced by Singleton after several days of shooting, simply because Singleton imparted more warmth to the character and handled the proceedings with more comedic flair. Of her co-star Arthur Lake, Singleton told this writer: "He was just born to be Dagwood. He was just perfect, I thought, and a nice person."

As the series progressed, though, maintaining an astonishingly faithful continuity as the Bumstead children grew and so on, the films began to lose energy and grow tiresome. The leads, too, were maturing, and Singleton in particular showed her age in the close-ups (she was already thirty years old in the first entry). By the time BLONDIE was adapted as a TV series in the early 1950s, with a now paunchy Lake still cavorting as Dagwood, Singleton had been replaced by Pamela Britton. Britton, although no match for Singleton in her prime, was quite good, but the series was not a success.

Even less successful was a much later 1968–69 incarnation on CBS, starring Patricia Harty and Will Hutchins. In the social turmoil of the late '60s, Chic Young's befuddled suburban couple seemed glaringly dated and sadly out of place. After only a few episodes, the show quickly folded and was immediately forgotten.

BRENDA STARR
newspaper strip

BRENDA STARR, REPORTER (Columbia, 1945)— theatrical serial; 13 chapters, first chapter approximately 30 minutes, remaining chapters approximately 20 minutes each.

Credits: Producer: Sam Katzman; Director: Wallace W. Fox; Screenplay: Andy Lamb, George H. Plympton; Camera: Ira H. Morgan; Music: Edward Kay; Editor: Charles Henkel; Assistant Director: Mel DeLay.

Cast: Joan Woodbury (Brenda Starr); Kane Richmond (Lt. Larry Farrel); Syd Saylor (Chuck Allen); Joe Devlin (Tim); George Meeker (Frank Smith); Wheeler Oakman (Joe Heller/

BRENDA STARR, REPORTER (Columbia, 1945): Joan Woodbury, Kane Richmond.

Lew Heller); Cay Forester (Vera Harvey); Marion Burns (Zelda); Lottie Harrison (Abretha); Ernie Adams (Charlie); Jack Ingram (Kruger); Anthony Warde (Muller); John Merton (Schultz); Billy Benedict (Pesky).

Chapter Titles: (1) Hot News; (2) The Blazing Trap; (3) Taken for a Ride; (4) A Ghost Walks; (5) The Big Boss Speaks; (6) Man Hunt; (7) Hideout of Terror; (8) Killer at Large; (9) Dark Magic; (10) A Double-Cross Backfires; (11) On the Spot; (12) Murder at Night; (13) The Mystery of the Payroll.

BRENDA STARR (NBC, 1976)—TV movie; 90 minutes; color.

Credits: Executive Producer: Paul Mason; Producer: Bob Larson; Director: Mel Stuart; Screenplay: George Kirgo; Camera: Ted Voightlander; Art Director: Art Tunkle; Music: Lalo Schifrin.

Cast: Jill St. John (Brenda Starr); Sorrell Booke (A. J. Livwright); Jed Allan (Roger Randall); Victor Buono (Lance O'Toole); Marcia Strassman (Kentucky Smith); Barbara Luna (Luisa Santamaria); Joel Fabiani (Carlos Varga); Tabi Cooper (Hank O'Hare); Torin Thatcher (Lassiter); Art Roberts (Leander); Roy Applegate (Tommy).

BRENDA STARR, REPORTER (Syndicated, 1979)—TV pilot; 30 minutes; color.

Credits: Producer: Jerry Harrison: Director: Lawrence Dobkin; Screenplay: Jerry Harrison; Music: Richard La Salle.

Cast: Sherry Jackson (Brenda Starr); Shelly Berman (A. J. Livwright).

BRENDA STARR (New World, 1989)—theatrical feature; 87 minutes; color.

Credits: Producer: Myron A. Hyman; Executive Producer: John D. Backe; Director: Robert Ellis Miller; Screenplay: Noreen Stone, James David Buchanan, Jenny Wolkind (Original Story: Noreen Stone, James David Buchanan); Camera: Freddie Francis; Editor: Mark Melnick; Music: Johnny Mandel; Sound: Sharon Smith-Holly; Costumes (for Brooke Shields): Bob Mackie; Costumes: Peggy Farrell; Animation Sequences: Japhet Asher, Colossal Pictures/USFX; Casting: Pat McCorakle.

Cast: Brooke Shields (Brenda Starr): Timothy Dalton (Basil St. John); Tony Peck (Mike Randall); Diana Scarwid (Libby "Lips" Lipscomb); Charles Durning (Newspaper Editor); Eddie Albert (Police Chief); Ed Nelson (President Truman); Nestor Serrano; Jeffrey Tambor; June Gable; Kathleen Wilhoite; John Short; Henry Gibson; Tom Aldredge; Matthew Cowles; Abner Eisenberg; Mary Lou Rosato; Anthony Jay Peck.

This adventure strip about a beautiful girl reporter was created by Dale Messick for the Chicago Tribune-New York News Syndicate, the first installment appearing in June of 1940. The Columbia Pictures serial based on the strip was more faithful to Messick's character than the negligible television incarnations of later years, or the recent feature starring Brooke Shields, which was so inept that the picture's release was delayed for nearly three years.

BRICK BRADFORD
newspaper strip

BRICK BRADFORD (Columbia, 1947)—theatrical serial; 15 chapters, first chapter approximately 30 minutes, remaining chapters approximately 20 minutes each.

BRICK BRADFORD (Columbia, 1947): Unknown Columbia starlet Linda Johnson and lead Kane Richmond.

Credits: Producer: Sam Katzman; Director: Spencer G. Bennet; Screenplay: George H. Plympton, Arthur Hoerl, Lewis Clay; Camera: Ira H. Morgan; Music: Mischa Bakaleinikoff; Editor: Earl Turner; Assistant Director: R. M. Andrews; Second Unit Director: Thomas Carr.

Cast: Kane Richmond (Brick Bradford); Rick Vallin (Sandy Sanderson); Linda Johnson (June Sanders); Pierre Watkin (Professor Salisbury); Charles Quigley (Laydron); Jack Ingram (Albers); Fred Graham (Black); John Merton (Dr. Tymak); Leonard Penn (Byrus); Wheeler Oakman (Walthar); Carol Forman (Queen Khana); Charles King (Creed); John Hart (Dent); Helene Stanley (Carol Preston); Nelson Leigh (Prescott); Robert Barron (Zontar); George DeNormand (Meaker); Noel Neill (Indian Girl).

Chapter Titles: (1) Atomic Defense; (2) Flight to the Moon; (3) Prisoners of the Moon; (4) Into the Volcano; (5) Bradford at Bay; (6) Back to Earth; (7) Into Another Century; (8) Buried Treasure; (9) Trapped in the Time Top; (10) The Unseen Hand; (11) Poison Gas; (12) Door of Disaster; (13) Sinister Rendezvous; (14) River of Revenge; (15) For the Peace of the World.

Somewhat derivative of BUCK ROGERS, this fantasy-adventure strip was created by writer William Ritt and artist William Gray for Central Press Association, with the first installment appearing in August of 1933. The strip was later distributed by King Features Syndicate, until it was discontinued in 1957. The Columbia Pictures serial based on the strip is another woefully impoverished effort from that studio's cliff-hanger maestro Sam Katzman. What could have been a lavish (at least by serial standards) fantasy in the same mold as Universal's FLASH GORDON becomes a thudding disappointment in the fumbling hands of Katzman, whose contempt for his audience is apparently boundless. Featuring almost non-existent special effects and a listless performance by the otherwise excellent Kane Richmond, BRICK BRADFORD is a major creative disaster on nearly every level. At one point in the narrative, Bradford is transported to the moon, and instead of a lunar milieu that is at least partially convincing, the viewer is presented with the tacky spectacle of Richmond scurrying about the familiar landscape of Bronson Canyon in broad daylight—with clouds plainly visible in the lunar sky! Richmond looks rather embarrassed throughout this forgettable chapterplay, and one can hardly blame him.

BRINGING UP FATHER (JIGGS AND MAGGIE)
newspaper strip

FATHER'S CLOSE SHAVE (Pathé, 1920)—theatrical short subject.

JIGGS AND THE SOCIAL LION (Pathé, 1920)—theatrical short subject.

JIGGS IN SOCIETY (Pathé, 1920)—theatrical short subject.

BRINGING UP FATHER (M-G-M, 1928)—theatrical feature; 62 minutes.

Credits: Director: Jack Conway; Titles: Ralph Spence; Camera: William Daniels.

Cast: Farrell MacDonald (Jiggs); Polly Moran (Maggie); Jules Cowles (Dinty Moore); Marie Dressler (Annie Moore); Gertrude Olmstead (Ellen); Grant Withers (Dennis); Andres de Segurola (The Count); Rose Dione (Mrs. Smith); David Mir (Oswald); Tenen Holtz (Fiedelbaum); Toto (Dog).

BRINGING UP FATHER (Monogram, 1946)—theatrical feature; 68 minutes.

Credits: Producer: Barney Gerard; Director: Eddie Cline; Screenplay: Jerry Warner (Original Story: Barney Gerard); Camera: L. W. O'Connell; Music: Edward Kay; Editor: Ralph Dixon.

Cast: Joe Yule (Jiggs); Renie Riano (Maggie); George McManus (Himself); Tim Ryan (Dinty Moore); June Harrison (Nora); Wallace Chadwell (Danny); Tom Kennedy (Kermishaw); Pat Goldin (Dugan); Tom Dugan (Hod Carrier); Joe Devlin (Casey); Fred Kelsey (Tom); Charles Wilson (Frank); Herbert Evans (Jenkins); Dick Ryan (Grogharty); Mike Pat Donovan (Jerry); Bob Carleton (Pianist); George Hickman (Fogarty).

JIGGS AND MAGGIE IN COURT (Monogram, 1948)— theatrical feature; 60 minutes.

Credits: Producer: Barney Gerard; Directors: William Beaudine, Eddie Cline; Screenplay: Barney Gerard, Eddie Cline.

Cast: Joe Yule; Renie Riano; June Harrison; Riley Hill; Tim Ryan; Robert Lowell; Pat Goldin; Danny Beck; Dick Ryan; Cliff Clark; George McManus; Jimmy Aubrey; Jean Fenwick; Frank Austin; Russell Hicks; Chester Clute; Grady Sutton; Sydney Marion; Charles Middleton; Richard R. Neill; Ken Britton; Francine Faye; Bobby Hale; Fred Kelsey; Jimmy O'Brien; Herman Cantor; Marie Harmon; Baron Lichter.

JIGGS AND MAGGIE IN SOCIETY (Monogram, 1948)—theatrical feature; 65 minutes.

Credits: Producer: Barney Gerard; Director: Eddie Cline; Screenplay: Eddie Cline, Barney Gerard; Camera: L. W. O'Connell; Music: Edward J. Kay; Art Director: Dave Milton; Editor: Ace Herman.

Cast: Joe Yule (Jiggs); Renie Riano (Maggie); Dale Carnegie (Himself); Arthur Murray (Himself); Sheilah Graham (Herself); Tim Ryan (Dinty Moore); Wanda McKay (Millicent); Lee Bonnell (Van De Graft); Pat Goldin (Dugan); Herbert Evans (Jenkins); June Harrison (Nora); Scott Taylor (Tommy); Jimmy Aubrey (McGurk); Thayer Roberts (Pete); Richard Irving (Al); William Cabanne (George); Dick Ryan (Grogan);

JIGGS AND MAGGIE IN SOCIETY (Monogram, 1948): An original theatre poster.

Constance Purdy (Mrs. Blackwell); Edith Leslie (Mary); Helena Dare (Aggie); Leslie Farley (Miami); Betty Blythe (Mrs. Vacuum); Marcelle Imhof (Mrs. Heavydoe).

JIGGS AND MAGGIE IN JACKPOT JITTERS (Monogram, 1949)—theatrical feature; 67 minutes.

Credits: Producer: Barney Gerard; Director: William Beaudine; Screenplay: Barney Gerard, Eddie Cline.

Cast: Joe Yule; Renie Riano; George McManus; Walter McCarthy; Tim Ryan; Jimmy Aubrey; Tom Kennedy; Betty Blythe; Ed East; Earle Hodgins; Willie Best; Sid Marion; Marcelle Imhof; Hank Mann; Chester Conklin; Leon Belasco; Eddie Kane; Sam Hayes; Joe Hernandez.

JIGGS AND MAGGIE OUT WEST (Monogram, 1950)— theatrical feature; 66 minutes.

Credits: Producer: Barney Gerard; Director: William Beaudine; Screenplay: Barney Gerard, Adele Buffington (Original Story by Barney Gerard and Eddie Cline); Camera: L. W. O'Connell; Music: Edward Kay; Art Director: Dave Milton; Editor: Roy V. Livingston.

Cast: Joe Yule (Jiggs); Renie Riano (Maggie); George McManus (Himself); Tim Ryan (Dinty Moore); Jim Bannon (Snake Bite); Riley Hill (Bob Carter); Pat Goldin (Dugan); June Harrison (Nora); Henry "Kulky" Kulkovich (Bomber); Terry McGinnis (Cyclone); Billy Griffith (Lawyer Blakely).

Created by George McManus for the Hearst Syndicate, the first installment of BRINGING UP FATHER appeared in 1913. Relating the misadventures of a nouveau-riche working-class couple, the strip immediately captured a large audience with its clever scripting and bizarre characters, as the social-climbing Maggie and her loutish but affable husband Jiggs found themselves in a continuous battle of the sexes. Aside from the 1928 M-G-M feature based on the strip, the other films based on McManus's characters have been negligible "B" pictures and shorts duplicating little of McManus's creativity, their success buoyed by the popularity of the strip. George McManus himself appeared in the Monogram features.

BRUCE GENTRY
newspaper strip

BRUCE GENTRY (Columbia, 1949)—theatrical serial; 15 chapters, first chapter approximately 30 minutes, remaining chapters approximately 20 minutes each.

Credits: Producer: Sam Katzman; Directors: Spencer G. Bennet, Thomas Carr; Screenplay: George H. Plympton, Joseph F. Poland, Lewis Clay; Camera: Ira H. Morgan; Music: Mischa Bakaleinikoff; Editors: Earl Turner, Dwight Caldwell; Assistant Director: R. M. Andrews.

Cast: Tom Neal (Bruce Gentry); Judy Clark (Juanita Farrell); Ralph Hodges (Frank Farrell); Forrest Taylor (Dr. Alexander Benson); Hugh Prosser (Paul Radcliffe); Tristram Coffin (Krendon); Jack Ingram (Allen); Terry Frost (Chandler); Eddie Parker (Gregg); Charles King (Ivor); Stephen Carr (Hill); Dale Van Sickle (Gregory).

Chapter Titles: (1) The Mystery Disc; (2) Fiery Furnace; (3) The Man of Menace; (4) Grade Crossing; (5) Danger Trail; (6) A Fight for Life; (7) The Flying Disc; (8) Fate Takes the Wheel;

(9) Hazardous Heights; (10) Over the Falls; (11) Gentry at Bay; (12) Parachute of Peril; (13) Menace of the Mesa; (14) Bruce's Strategy; (15) The Final Disc.

This aviation-adventure strip was created by Ray Bailey for the Hall Syndicate, and first appeared in March of 1945, running until it was cancelled in 1952. The Columbia Pictures serial based on the strip was not one of the studio's better efforts.

BUCK ROGERS
newspaper strip

BUCK ROGERS (Universal, 1939)—theatrical serial; 12 chapters, approximately 20 minutes each.

Credits: Associate Producer: Barney Sarecky; Directors: Ford Beebe, Saul Goodkind; Screenplay: Norman S. Hall, Ray Trampe; Camera: Jerry Ash; Art Direction: Jack Otterson, Ralph DeLacy.

Cast: Larry "Buster" Crabbe (Buck Rogers); Constance Moore (Wilma Deering); Jackie Moran (Buddy Wade); Jack Mulhall (Captain Rankin); Anthony Warde (Killer Kane); C. Montague Shaw (Dr. Huer); Guy Usher (Aldar); William Gould (Marshall Kragg); Philson Ahn (Prince Tallen); Henry Brandon (Captain Lasca); Wheeler Oakman (Patten); Kenneth Duncan (Lieutenant Lacy); Carleton Yound (Scott); Reed Howes (Roberts).

Chapter Titles: (1) Tomorrow's World; (2) Tragedy on Saturn; (3) The Enemy's Stronghold; (4) The Sky Patrol; (5) The Phantom Plane; (6) The Unknown Command; (7) The Primitive Urge; (8) Revolt of the Zuggs; (9) Bodies Without Minds; (10) Broken Barriers; (11) A Prince in Bondage; (12) War of the Planets.

BUCK ROGERS (Universal, 1939): Buster Crabbe, *right,* in a tense situation.

Note: Two different feature-length versions have been re-edited from this serial: PLANET OUTLAWS, for theatrical distribution, and DESTINATION SATURN, for TV syndication.

BUCK ROGERS IN THE 25TH CENTURY (ABC, 1950–51)—TV series; each episode 30 minutes.

Credits: Producers: Joseph Cates, Babette Henry; Director: Babette Henry; Series Writer: Gene Wyckoff.

Cast: Kem Dibbs, Robert Pastene (Buck Rogers); Lou Prentis (Lt. Wilma Deering); Harry Southern (Dr. Huer); Harry Kingston (Black Barney Wade); Sanford Bickard.

BUCK ROGERS IN THE 25TH CENTURY (Universal, 1979)—theatrical feature; 89 minutes; color.

Credits: Producer: Richard Caffey; Director: Daniel Haller; Screenplay: Glen A. Larson, Leslie Stevens; Camera: Frank Beascoecher; Music: Stu Phillips; Editor: John Dumas; Costumes: Jean-Pierre Dorleac; Choreographer: Miriam Nelson.

Cast: Gil Gerard (Buck Rogers); Pamela Hensley (Princess Ardala); Erin Gray (Wilma Deering); Henry Silva (Kane); Tim O'Connor (Dr. Huer); Joseph Wiseman (Draco); Duke Butler (Tigerman); Felix Sila (Twiki); Mel Blanc (Twiki's Voice); Caroline Smith (Young Woman); John Dewey-Carter (Supervisor); Kevin Coates (Pilot); David Cadiente (Comtel Officer); Gil Serna (Technician); Larry Duran, Kenny Endosoa (Guards); Eric Lawrence (Officer); H. B. Haggerty (Tigerman Two); Coleen Kelly (Wrather); Steve Jones, David Buchanan (Pilots); Burt Marshall (Wing Man).

BUCK ROGERS IN THE 25TH CENTURY (NBC, 1979–81)—TV Series; 33 episodes, 60 minutes each; color.

Credits: Executive Producers: Glen A. Larson, John Mantley; Supervising Producers: Leslie Stevens, Bruce Lansbury, Calvin Clements; Producers: Richard Caffey, John Gaynor, David J. O'Connell, John G. Stephens; Series Directors: Daniel Haller, Michael Caffey, Sigmund Neufeld, Jr., Dick Lowry, Philip Leacock, Leslie H. Martinson, David Moessinger, Larry Stewart, David Phinney, Vincent McEveety, Victor French, Bernard McEveety, Jack Arnold, Barry Crane, John Patterson; Camera: Ben Colman; Art Directors: Bill Camden, Fred Luff, Hub Braden, Fred Camden, William Tuntke; Music: Stu Phillips, Les Baxter, Johnny Harris, J. J. Johnson, John Cacavas, Herbert Woods, Bruce Broughton, Donald Woods; Theme: Glen A. Larson.

Cast: Gil Gerard (Capt. William "Buck" Rogers); Erin Gray (Lt. Wilma Deering); Tim O'Connor (Dr. Elias Huer); Wilfred Hyde-White (Dr. Goodfellow); Jay Garner (Admiral Efrem Asimov); Felix Silla (Twiki); Thom Christopher (Hawk); Barbara Luna (Koovi); Pamela Hensley (Princess Ardella); Henry Silva, Michael Ansara (Kane); Duke Butler, H. B. Haggerty (Tigerman); Mel Blanc (Voice of Twiki); Eric Server (Voice of Dr. Theopolis); Jeff David (Voice of Crichton); Paul Carr (Lieutenant Davis); Alex Hyde-White (Lieutenant Moore).

Created by writer Phil Nowlan from his novel *Armageddon 2419* and drawn by Dick Calkins, BUCK ROGERS is the first American science-fiction comic strip and undeniably the most influential. Distributed by the John F. Dille Co., the first installment appeared in January of 1929, the strip running until it was discontinued in 1967. In terms of physical detail, the Universal serial based on the strip is one of the studio's more ambitious efforts, but it remains oddly unsatisfying and uninvolving, probably because the scriptwriters failed to bring much depth to the characters, and also because Buster Crabbe, after two FLASH GORDON serials for the same studio, was just too identified with that rival character. The conclusion, too, is unforgivably weak, with Crabbe, after leading a conquering army of rebels to decisive victory against villain Killer Kane's hordes (in an apocalyptic battle that conveniently takes place off-screen), running into Kane's inner sanctum totally unopposed by any bodyguards or soldiers and smugly declaring "You're through, Kane— better give up!" The strip also spawned a tacky early TV series, broadcast live on ABC, and the much-later NBC series starring Gil Gerard and Erin Gray, which had more in common with STAR WARS than the original strip or serial.

BUSTER BROWN
newspaper strip

BUSTER BROWN—theatrical short subjects.

The following two-reel comedies were released by Universal Pictures. These titles have been confirmed as BUSTER BROWN shorts, although there may have been additional titles that are unknown.

BUSTER BE GOOD (1925); BUSTER'S BUST-UP (1925); BUSTER'S HUNTING PARTY (1925); EDUCATING BUSTER (1925); BUSTER, DON'T FORGET (1926); BUSTER HELPS DAD (1926); BUSTER, WATCH TIGE (1926); BUSTER'S DARK MYSTERY (1926); BUSTER'S GIRL FRIEND (1926); BUSTER'S HEART-BEATS (1926); BUSTER'S MIX-UP (1926); BUSTER'S NARROW ESCAPE (1926); BUSTER'S ORPHAN PARTY (1926); BUSTER'S PICNIC (1926); BUSTER'S PRIZE WINNER (1926); BUSTER'S SLEIGH RIDE (1926); BUSTER COME ON (1927); BUSTER SHOWS OFF (1927); BUSTER STEPS OUT (1927); BUSTER, WHAT NEXT? (1927); BUSTER'S BIG CHANCE (1927); BUSTER'S FRAME-UP (1927); BUSTER'S HANDICAP (1927); BUSTER'S HOME LIFE (1927); BUSTER'S INITIATION (1927); RUN BUSTER (1927); BUSTER MINDS THE BABY (1928); BUSTER TRIMS UP (1928); BUSTING BUSTER (1928); BUSTER'S WHIPPET RACE (1928); GOOD SCOUT BUSTER (1928); HALF-BACK BUSTER (1928); HAVE PATIENCE (1928); KNOCKOUT BUSTER (1928); OUT AT HOME (1928); TEACHER'S PEST (1928); WATCH THE BIRDIE (1928); BUSTER'S SPOOKS (1929); DELIVERING THE GOODS (1929); GETTING BUSTER'S GOAT (1929); MAGIC (1929); TIGE'S GIRL FRIEND (1929).

Created by R. F. Outcalt for the *New York Herald* in 1902, this strip related the humorous misadventures of a wealthy suburban family's ten-year-old son and his pet bulldog, Tige. Wildly popular, the strip was bought (after a legal battle) by Hearst's *New York American* in 1906, where it ran until 1920. The Buster Brown character itself continued beyond the strip, remaining popular through advertising use and book reprints of the old strips. The Stern brothers, producers at Universal Pictures intent on creating a comedy series to rival Hal Roach's famous OUR GANG films, first created the BABY PEGGY series, then a series of shorts based on THE NEWLYWEDS (q.v.) comic strip. Both were only mild successes, but the Sterns really clicked with their third attempt, the BUSTER BROWN series, based on Outcalt's strip and starring Doreen Turner as Buster with Pete the Pup as Tige. Several of these two-reel shorts were filmed in the 1920s, and a few of them were later syndicated to television (along with other films) under the umbrella title THE MISCHIEF MAKERS. The directors were Gus Meins and Francis Corby, who later, ironically, directed OUR GANG shorts for Hal Roach.

CAPTAIN AMERICA
comic book
Timely/Marvel Comics

CAPTAIN AMERICA (Republic, 1944)—theatrical serial; 15 chapters, first chapter approximately 30 minutes, remaining chapters approximately 20 minutes each.

Credits: Associate Producer: William J. O'Sullivan; Directors: John English, Elmer Clifton; Screenplay: Royal Cole, Ronald

CAPTAIN AMERICA (Republic, 1944): Dick Purcell, *right,* delivers a sluggish blow to an opponent.

Davidson, Basil Dickey, Jesse Duffy, Harry Fraser, Grant Nelson, Joseph Poland; Camera: John McBurnie; Music: Mort Glickman; Special Effects: Theodore Lydecker.

Cast: Dick Purcell (Captain America/Grant Gardner); Lorna Gray (Gail Richards); Lionel Atwill (Dr. Maldor); Charles Trowbridge (Commissioner Dryden); Russell Hicks (Mayor Randolph); George J. Lewis (Matson); John Davidson (Gruber); Norman Nesbitt (Newscaster); Frank Reicher (Professor Lyman); Hugh Sothern (Professor Dodge); Tom Chatterton (Henley); Robert Frazer (Dr. Clinton Lyman); John Hamilton (Hillman); Crane Whitley (Dirk); Edward Keane (Dr. Baracs); John Bagni (Monk); Jay Novello (Simms).

Chapter Titles: The Purple Death; (2) Mechanical Executioner; (3) The Secret Shroud; (4) Preview of Murder; (5) Blade of Wrath; (6) Vault of Vengeance; (7) Wholesale Destruction; (8) Cremation in the Clouds; (9) Triple Tragedy; (10) The Avenging Corpse; (11) The Dead Man Returns; (12) Horror on the Highway; (13) Skyscraper Plunge; (14) The Scarab Strikes; (15) The Toll of Doom.

Note: The serial was reissued as THE RETURN OF CAPTAIN AMERICA.

CAPTAIN AMERICA (CBS, 1979)—TV movie; 120 minutes; color.

Credits: Executive Producer: Alan Balter; Producer: Martin Goldstein; Director: Rod Holcomb; Screenplay: Don Ingalls; Camera: Roland W. Browne; Art Director: Lou Montejano; Music: Mike Post, Pete Carpenter.

Cast: Reb Brown (Captain America/Steve Rogers); Len Birman (Dr. Simon Mills); Heather Menzies (Dr. Wendy Day); Steve Forrest (Lou Brackett); Lance Le Gault (Harley); Frank Marth (Charles Barber); Joseph Ruskin (Sandrini); Dan Barton (Jeff Hayden); James Ingersol (Lester Wayne); Jason Wingreen (Sergeant); June Dayton (Secretary); Michael McManus (Ortho).

CAPTAIN AMERICA (CBS, 1979)—TV movie; 120 minutes; color.

Credits: Executive Producer: Alan Balter; Producer: Martin Goldstein; Director: Ivan Nagy; Screenplay: Wilton Schiller, Patricia Payne; Music: Mike Post, Peter Carpenter.

Cast: Reb Brown (Captain America/Steve Rogers); Len Birman (Dr. Simon Mills); Connie Sellecca (Dr. Wendy Day); Christopher Lee (Miguel); Lana Wood (Yolanda); Katherin Justice (Heflin); Christopher Cary (Professor Ilson); John Waldron (Peter Moore); June Dayton (June Cullen); William Mims (Dr. J. Brenner).

Note: This film was originally broadcast in two separate one-hour segments.

Created by writer Joe Simon and artist Jack Kirby, CAPTAIN AMERICA first appeared in CAPTAIN AMERICA #1 in March of 1941. A flagrantly patriotic creation that barely managed to survive World War II, the book limped along after the war until it was discontinued in 1949. It was briefly revived in 1954 only to be met with disinterest and was discontinued again that same year. CAPTAIN AMERICA was again revived in AVENGERS #4 in March of 1964, this time successfully, and was again given his own book. Although the Republic Pictures serial adaptation of the strip had little to do with its inspiration, changing the name of Captain America's alter ego from Steve Rogers to Grant Gardner, transforming him from an Army private to a crusading district attorney, altering the character's costume and eliminating his juvenile assistant Bucky and the wartime milieu entirely, the film is still great fun on its own terms. This serial offers fifteen chapters of genial, almost non-stop mayhem as trigger-happy D.A. Grant Gardner and his equally gun-crazed girl assistant shoot first and ask questions later as they oppose the nefarious schemes of the villainous Scarab. The gunplay and violence reach such unintentionally ludicrous heights that all of the somehow bloodless mayhem becomes somewhat cartoonish and inoffensive, and the serial, despite its infidelities to the original strip, was still a good deal more faithful than the two much later unbelievably inept TV movies.

CAPTAIN MARVEL
comic book
Fawcett Publications

THE ADVENTURES OF CAPTAIN MARVEL (Republic, 1941)—theatrical serial; 12 chapters, first chapter approximately 30 minutes, remaining chapters approximately 20 minutes each.

Credits: Associate Producer: Hiram S. Brown, Jr.; Directors: William Witney, John English; Screenplay: Sol Shor, Ronald Davidson, Norman S. Hall, Joseph Poland, Arch B. Heath; Camera: William Nobles; Music: Cy Feuer.

Cast: Tom Tyler (Captain Marvel); Frank Coghlan, Jr. (Billy Batson); William Benedict (Whitey); Louis Currie (Betty Wallace); Robert Strange (John Malcolm); Harry Worth (Professor Bentley); Bryant Washburn (Harry Carlyle); John Davidson (Tal Chotali); George Pembroke (Dr. Stephen Lang); Peter George Lynn (Dwight Fisher); Reed Hadley (Rahman Bar); Jack Mulhall (Howell); Kenneth Duncan (Barnett); Nigel de Brulier (Shazam); John Bagni (Cowan); Carleton Young (Martin); Leland Hodgson (Major Rawley); Stanley Price (Owens); Ernest Sarracino (Akbar); Tetsu Komai (Chan Lai).

Chapter Titles: (1) Curse of the Scorpion; (2) The Guillotine; (3) Time Bomb; (4) Death Takes the Wheel; (5) The Scorpion Strikes; (6) Lens of Death; (7) Human Targets; (8) Boomerang; (9) Dead Man's Trap; (10) Doom Ship; (11) Valley of Death; (12) Captain Marvel's Secret.

Note: This serial was reissued as THE RETURN OF CAPTAIN MARVEL.

THE ADVENTURES OF CAPTAIN MARVEL (Republic, 1941): Tom Tyler in the title role.

SHAZAM! (CBS, 1974–77)—TV series; each episode 30 minutes; color.

Credits: Executive Producers: Norm Prescott, Lou Scheimer, Dick Rosenbloom; Music: Yvette Blais, Jeff Michael.

Cast: Jackson Bostwick (Captain Marvel, First Season); John Davey (Captain Marvel, Second Season); Michael Gray (Billy Batson); Les Tremayne (Mentor).

Originally entitled CAPTAIN THUNDER (although this incarnation never saw print and was drawn only to secure copyrights), CAPTAIN MARVEL was created by writer Bill Parker and artist C. C. Beck for WHIZ COMICS #1 in February of 1940.

Designed as a blatant SUPERMAN imitation, and ultimately sued out of existence by the publishers of SUPERMAN, CAPTAIN MARVEL, in its print version, was in many ways a more charming and more carefully formulated character than its rival. The creators of CAPTAIN MARVEL, fully aware that the children who read comic books at that time subconsciously wished to become those heroic characters, invented an adult character who was, in reality, a child. Drawn to resemble actor Fred MacMurray, Captain Marvel was actually young Billy Batson who, by invoking the name of Shazam, an ancient deity, was temporarily granted a muscular adult body endowed with superhuman powers.

Republic Pictures' serial adaptation took a more prosaic, "realistic" approach than the comparatively juvenile comic book, but was one of the studio's better serials, featuring some impressive flying effects.

CONGO BILL
comic book

CONGO BILL (Columbia, 1948)—theatrical serial; 15 chapters, first chapter approximately 30 minutes, remaining chapters approximately 20 minutes each.

Credits: Producer: Sam Katzman; Directors: Spencer G. Bennet, Thomas Carr; Screenplay: George H. Plympton, Arthur Hoerl, Lewis Clay; Camera: Ira H. Morgan; Music: Mischa Bakaleinikoff; Editors: Earl Turner, Dwight Caldwell; Assistant Director: R. M. Andrews.

Cast: Don McGuire (Congo Bill); Cleo Moore (Lureen); Jack Ingram (Cameron); I. Stanford Jolley (Bernie MacGraw); Leonard Penn (André Bocar); Nelson Leigh (Dr. Greenway); Charles King (Kleeg); Armida (Zalea); Hugh Prosser (Morelli); Neyle Morrow (Kahla); Fred Graham (Villabo); Rusty Wescoatt (Ivan); Anthony Warde (Rogan); Stephen Carr (Tom MacGraw).

Chapter Titles: (1) The Untamed Beast; (2) Jungle Gold; (3) A Hot Reception; (4) Congo Bill Springs a Trap; (5) White Shadows in the Jungle; (6) The White Queen; (7) The Black Panther; (8) Sinister Schemes; (9) The Witch Doctor Strikes; (10) Trail of Treachery; (11) A Desparate Chance; (12) The Lair of the Beast; (13) Menace of the Jungle; (14) Treasure Trap; (15) The Missing Letter.

This derivative jungle hero premiered in ACTION COMICS #37 in 1942, spawning a forgettable Columbia Pictures serial six years later. Lacking any originality whatsoever, the character, never more than a back-up feature for SUPERMAN, steadily declined in popularity until a bizarre last-ditch attempt to revamp CONGO BILL was made with issue #248 of ACTION. The feature was retitled CONGORILLA, and the first installment of the new version found Congo Bill discovering a magical ring which, when rubbed, endowed the adventurer with the dubious power of switching his mind with that of a golden-haired gorilla, using his intelligence in combination with the beast's strength in order to battle jungle injustice. Unfortunately, this mental transference also left Congo Bill's body in possession of the gorilla's brain, resulting in the incongruous sight of the now-intelligent ape frequently restraining his now-bestial human counterpart by tying him to a tree until whatever adventure of the moment was concluded. This new incarnation of the strip only lasted until issue #280 until it was mercifully retired for good. Unfortunately, Sam Katzman and Columbia Pictures were never inclined to film CONGORILLA, much to the regret of bad-film lovers everywhere.

DENNIS THE MENACE
newspaper strip

DENNIS THE MENACE (CBS, 1959–63)—TV series; 146 episodes, 30 minute each.

Credits: Executive Producer: Harry Ackerman; Producers: Winston O'Keefe, James Fonda; Series Directors: Charles Barton, William D. Russell, Norman Abbott, Don Taylor, James Goldstone; Music: Irving Friedman.

Cast: Jay North (Dennis Mitchell); Herbert Anderson (Henry Mitchell); Gloria Henry (Alice Mitchell); Joseph Kearns (George Wilson); Sylvia Field (Martha Wilson); Gale Gordon (John Wilson); Sara Seeger (Eloise Wilson); Billy Booth (Tommy Anderson); Robert John Pitman (Seymour Williams); Jeannie Russell (Margaret Wade); George Cisar (Sgt. Theodore Mooney); Irene Tedrow (Mrs. Lucy Elkins); Willard Waterman (Mr. Quigley); Charles Lane (Lawrence Finch); Robert B. Williams (Mr. Dorfman); Gil Smith (Joey MacDonald); Mary Wickes (Esther Cathcart); Henry Norell (James Trask); J. Edward McKinley (Mr. Hall); Byron Foulger (Mr. Timberlake); Will Wright (Mr. Merivale); Nancy Evans (June Wilson); Edward Everett Horton (Ned Matthews); Elinor Donahue (Georgianna Ballinger); Charles Seel (Mr. Krinkle);

Charles Watts (Mayor Yates); Kathleen Mulqueen (Henry's Mother); James Beil (Grandpa Perkins); Verna Felton (Aunt Emma); Alice Pearce (Lucy Tarbell).

Created by Hank Ketchum, this humor strip, distributed by the Hall Syndicate, first appeared in March of 1951. The popularity of Ketchum's spoiled brat child character is difficult to fathom, but the strip has been a continuous success, and the TV incarnation remained popular for several years.

DESPERATE DESMOND
newspaper strip

See MUTT & JEFF for details.

DICK TRACY
newspaper strip

DICK TRACY (Republic, 1937)—theatrical serial; 15 chapters, first chapter approximately 30 minutes, remaining chapters approximately 20 minutes each.

Credits: Associate Producer: J. Laurence Wickland; Directors: Ray Taylor, Alan James; Screenplay: Barry Shipman, Winston Miller (Original Story: Morgan Cox, George Morgan); Camera: William Nobles, Edgar Lyons; Music: Harry Grey.

Cast: Ralph Byrd (Dick Tracy); Kay Hughes (Gwen); Smiley Burnette (Mike McGurk); Lee Van Atta (Junior); John Piccori (Moloch); Carleton Young (Gordon Tracy, after); Fred Hamilton (Steve); Francis X. Bushman (Anderson); John Dilson

(Brewster); Richard Beach (Gordon Tracy, before); Wedge-wood Nowell (Clayton); Theodore Lorch (Paterno); Edwin Stanley (Odette); Harrison Greene (Cloggerstein); Herbert Weber (Martino); Buddy Roosevelt (Burke); George DeNormand (Flynn); Byron K. Foulger (Korvitch); Oscar, Elmer (Themselves).

Chapter Titles: (1) The Spider Strikes; (2) The Bridge of Terror; (3) The Fur Pirates; (4) Death Rides the Sky; (5) Brother Against Brother; (6) Dangerous Waters; (7) The Ghost Town Mystery; (8) Battle in the Clouds; (9) The Stratosphere Adventure; (10) The Gold Ship; (11) Harbor Pursuit; (12) The Trail of the Spider; (13) The Fire Trap; (14) The Devil in White; (15) Brothers United.

DICK TRACY RETURNS (Republic, 1938)—theatrical serial; 15 chapters, first chapter approximately 30 minutes, remaining chapters approximately 20 minutes each.

Credits: Associate Producer: Robert Beche; Directors: William Witney, John English; Screenplay: Barry Shipman, Franklyn Adreon, Ronald Davidson, Rex Taylor, Sol Shor; Camera: William Nobles; Music: Alberto Columbo.

Cast: Ralph Byrd (Dick Tracy); Lynn Roberts (Gwen); Charles Middleton (Pa Stark); Jerry Tucker (Junior); David Sharpe (Ron Merton); Lee Ford (Mike McGurk); Michael Kent (Steve); John Merton (Champ); Raphael Bennett (Trigger); Jack Roberts (Dude); Ned Glass (The Kid); Edward Foster (Joe Hanner); Alan Gregg (Snub); Reed Howes (Rance); Robert Terry (Reynolds); Tom Seidel (Hunt); Jack Ingram (Slasher).

Chapter Titles: (1) The Sky Wreckers; (2) The Runway of Death; (3) Handcuffed to Doom; (4) Four Seconds to Live; (5) Death in the Air; (6) Stolen Secrets; (7) Tower of Death; (8) Cargo of Destruction; (9) The Clock of Doom; (10) High

DICK TRACY RETURNS (Republic, 1938): Ralph Byrd, *center,* as Chester Gould's sleuth.

Voltage; (11) The Kidnapped Witness; (12) The Runaway Torpedo; (13) Passengers to Doom; (14) In the Hands of the Enemy; (15) G-Men's Dragnet.

DICK TRACY'S G-MEN (Republic, 1939)—theatrical serial; 15 chapters, first chapter approximately 30 minutes, remaining chapters approximately 20 minutes each.

Credits: Associate Producer: Robert Beche; Directors: William Witney, John English; Screenplay: Barry Shipman, Franklyn Adreon, Rex Taylor, Ronald Davidson, Sol Shor; Camera: William Nobles; Music: William Lava.

Cast: Ralph Byrd (Dick Tracy); Irving Pichel (Zarnoff); Ted Pearson (Steve); Phyllis Isley (Gwen); Walter Miller (Robal);

George Douglas (Sandoval); Kenneth Harlan (Anderson); Robert Carson (Scott); Julian Madison (Foster); Ted Mapes (First G-Man); William Stahl (Second G-Man); Robert Wayne (Third G-Man); Joe McGuinn (Tommy); Kenneth Terrell (Ed); Harry Humphrey (Warden Stover); Harrison Greene (Baron).

Chapter Titles: (1) The Master Spy; (2) Captured; (3) The False Signal; (4) The Enemy Strikes; (5) Crack up!; (6) Sunken Peril; (7) Tracking the Enemy; (8) Chamber of Doom; (9) Flames of Jeopardy; (10) Crackling Fury; (11) Caverns of Peril; (12) Fight in the Sky; (13) The Fatal Ride; (14) Getaway; (15) The Last Stand.

DICK TRACY VS. CRIME, INC. (Republic, 1941)— theatrical serial; 15 chapters, first chapter approximately 30 minutes, remaining chapters approximately 20 minutes each.

Credits: Associate Producer: William J. O'Sullivan; Directors: William Witney, John English; Screenplay: Ronald Davidson, Norman S. Hall, William Lively, Joseph O'Donnell, Joseph Poland; Camera: Reggie Lanning; Music: Cy Feuer; Special Effects: Howard Lydecker.

Cast: Ralph Byrd (Dick Tracy); Michael Owen (Billy Car); Jan Wiley (June Chandler); John Davidson (Lucifer); Ralph Morgan (Morton); Kenneth Harlan (Lieutenant Cosgrove); John Dilson (Weldon); Howard Hickman (Chandler); Robert Frazer (Brewster); Robert Fiske (Cabot); Jack Mulhall (Wilson); Hooper Atchley (Trent); Anthony Warde (Corey); Chuck Morrison (Trask).

Chapter Titles: (1) The Fatal Hour; (2) The Prisoner Vanishes; (3) Doom Patrol; (4) Dead Man's Trap; (5) Murder at Sea; (6) Besieged; (7) Sea Racketeers; (8) Train of Doom; (9) Beheaded; (10) Flaming Peril; (11) Seconds to Live; (12) Trial by Fire; (13) The Challenge; (14) Invisible Terror; (15) Retribution.

Note: This serial was reissued as DICK TRACY VS. THE PHANTOM EMPIRE.

DICK TRACY (RKO, 1945)—theatrical feature; 61 minues (*a.k.a.* DICK TRACY, DETECTIVE; *GB:* SPLITFACE).

Credits: Producer: Herman Schlom; Director: William Berke; Screenplay: Eric Taylor; Camera: Frank Redman; Music: Roy Webb; Editor: Ernie Leadway; Music: Constantin Bakaleinikoff; Art Directors: Albert S. D'Agostino, Ralph Berger; Set Design: Darrel Silvera, Jean L. Speak.

Cast: Morgan Conway (Dick Tracy); Anne Jeffreys (Tess Trueheart); Mike Mazurki (Splitface); Jane Greer (Judith Owens); Lyle Latell (Pat Patton); Joseph Crehan (Chief Brandon); Mickey Kuhn (Tracy, Jr.); Trevor Bardette (Professor Starling); Morgan Wallace (Steven Owens); Milton Parsons (Deathridge); William Halligan (Mayor); Edythe Elliot (Mrs. Caraway); Mary Currier (Dorothy Stafford); Ralph Dunn (Manning); Edmund Glover (Radio Announcer); Bruce Edwards (Sergeant); Tanis Chandler (Miss Stanley); Jimmy Jordan, Carl Hanson (Pedestrians); Franklin Farnum (Bystander at Murder); Jack Gargan, Sam Ash, Carl Faulkner, Frank Meredith, Bob Reeves (Cops); Tom Noonan (Johnny Moko); Harry Strang, George Magrill (Detectives); Robert Douglass (Busboy); Alphonse Martell (Jules, the Waiter); Gertrude Astor (Woman); Jack Chefe (Headwaiter); Florence Pepper (Girl); Wilbur Mack, Jason Robards, Sr. (Motorists).

DICK TRACY VS. CUEBALL (RKO, 1946)—theatrical feature; 62 minutes.

Credits: Producer: Herman Schlom; Director: Gordon M. Douglas; Screenplay: Dane Lussier, Robert E. Kent (Original Story: Luci Ward); Camera: George E. Diskant; Music:

Constantin Bakaleinikoff, Phil Oman; Editor: Philip Martin, Jr.; Art Director: Albert D'Agostino, Lucius O. Croxton; Set Design: Darrell Silvera, Shelby Willis.

Cast: Morgan Conway (Dick Tracy); Anne Jeffreys (Tess Trueheart); Lyle Latell (Pat Patton); Rita Corday (Mona Clyde); Ian Keith (Vitamin Flintheart); Dick Wessel (Cueball); Douglas Walton (Priceless); Esther Howard (Filthy Flora); Joseph Crehan (Chief Brandon); Byron Foulger (Little); Jimmy Crane (Junior); Milton Parsons (Higby); Skelton Knaggs (Rudolph); Ralph Dunn (Cop); Harry Cheshire (Jules Sprakle); Trevor Bardette (Lester Abbott).

DICK TRACY MEETS GRUESOME (RKO, 1947)— theatrical feature; 65 minutes (*a.k.a.* DICK TRACY MEETS KARLOFF; *GB:* DICK TRACY'S AMAZING ADVENTURE).

Credits: Producer: Herman Schlom; Director: John Rawlins; Screenplay: Robertson White, Eric Taylor (Original Story: William H. Graffis, Robert E. Kent); Camera: Frank Redman; Music: Paul Sawtell; Editor: Elmo Williams; Music: Constantin Bakaleinikoff; Art Directors: Albert S. D'Agostino, Walter Keller; Special Effects: Russell A. Cully.

Cast: Boris Karloff (Gruesome); Ralph Byrd (Dick Tracy); Anne Gwynne (Tess Trueheart); Edward Ashley (L. E. Thal); June Clayworth (Dr. I. M. Learned); Lyle Latell (Pat Patton); Tony Barrett (Melody); Skelton Knaggs (X-Ray); Jim Nolan (Dan Sterne); Joseph Crehan (Chief Brandon); Milton Parsons (Dr. A. Tomic); Lex Barker; Lee Phelps; Sean McClory; Harry Harvey; Harry Strang.

DICK TRACY'S DILEMMA (RKO, 1947)—theatrical feature; 60 minutes (*GB:* MARK OF THE CLAW).

Credits: Producer: Herman Schlom; Director: John Rawlins; Screenplay: Robert Stephen Brode; Camera: Frank Redman; Music: Paul Sawtell; Editor: Marvin Coll; Art Directors: Albert S. D'Agostino, Lucius O. Croxton.

Cast: Ralph Byrd (Dick Tracy); Kay Christopher (Tess Trueheart); Lyle Latell (Pat Patton); Jack Lambert (The Claw); Ian Keith (Vitamin Flintheart); Bernadene Hayes (Longshot Lillie); Jimmy Conlin (Sightless); William B. Davidson (Peter Premium); Tony Barrett (Sam); Richard Powers (Pred); Harry Strang (Night Watchman); Tom London (Cop in Squad Car); Jason Robards, Sr. (Watchman); Harry Harvey (Donovan the Cop); Sean McClory (Cop); Al Bridge (Police Detective); William Gould (Police Technician).

DICK TRACY (ABC, 1950–51)—TV series; each episode 30 minutes.

Credits: Producers: Dick Moore, P. K. Palmer, Keith Kalmer; Director: P. K. Palmer; Series Writer: P. K. Palmer.

Cast: Ralph Byrd (Dick Tracy); Joe Devlin (Sam Catchem); Angela Greene (Tess Trueheart); Dick Elliott (Police Chief Murphy).

DICK TRACY (Buena Vista, 1990)—theatrical feature; 103 minutes.

Credits: Executive Producers: Barrie M. Osborne, Art Linson, Floyd Mutrux; Producer/Director: Warren Beatty; Screenplay: Jim Cash, Jack Epps, Jr.; Photography (Technicolor): Vittorio Storano; Film Editor: Richard Marks; Music: Danny Elfman; Songs: Stephen Sondheim; Sound: Thomas Causey; Production Design: Richard Sylbert; Art Direction: Harold Michelson;

Set Decoration: Rick Simpson; Costume Design: Milena Canonero; Visual Effects: Buena Vista Visual Effects Group; Special Character Makeup: John Caglione, Jr., Doug Drexler; Choreography: Jeffrey Hornaday; Assistant Director/ Associate Producer: Jim Van Wyck; Second Unit Directors: Billy Burton, Richard Marks, Barrie M. Osborne; Second Unit Photography: James M. Anderson; Casting: Jackie Burch.

Cast: Warren Beatty (Dick Tracy); Charlie Korsmo (Kid); Glenne Headly (Tess Truehart); Madonna (Breathless Mahoney); Al Pacino (Big Boy Caprice); Dustin Hoffman (Mumbles); William Forsythe (Flat Top); Charles Durning (Chief Brandon); Mandy Patinkin (88 Keys); Paul Sorvino (Lips Manlis); R. G. Armstrong (Pruneface); Dick Van Dyke (D. A. Fletcher); Seymour Cassel; James Keane; Allen Garfield; John Shuck; Charles Fleischer; James Tolkan; Kathy Bates; Catherine O'Hara; Henry Silva; James Caan; Bert Remsen; Frank Campanella; Michael J. Pollard; Estelle Parsons; Mary Woronov; Henry Jones; Mike Mazurki.

Originally entitled PLAINCLOTHES TRACY by creator Chester Gould, this famous police-adventure strip, distributed by the Chicago Tribune-New York News Syndicate, premiered in October of 1931.

Republic Pictures, in adapting the Gould character for serial use, eschewed the flamboyant Gould idiom in favor of a more "realistic" approach. The colorful villains of the strip (Flat Top, Pruneface, etc.) were ignored, and the end result was, if not entirely faithful to Gould, then certainly acceptable cliffhanger fare.

Of the Republic DICK TRACY serials, DICK TRACY VS. CRIME, INC. is by far the best of the lot. When RKO adapted the character for several later "B" features, the resulting films were more faithful to the Gould strip, and also a good deal more light-hearted and comedic as a result. These pictures were all enjoyable on their own undemanding level, but the entry that by all rights should have been the best, DICK TRACY MEETS GRUESOME, with Boris Karloff as the titular fiend, was something of a misfire.

An unsold network TV pilot was filmed in the mid-60s by the producers of the Adam West BATMAN TV series.

The multi-million-dollar Warren Beatty production of 1990, despite its gargantuan cost and star cast, was a confused, generally lackluster affair. Whereas the previous serials and features (lacking huge budgets and stars) achieved their simple (and honest) goal of drawing and holding an audience, director/star Beatty (a bit old to play Tracy) felt it necessary to justify his production on both artistic and sociological grounds, a failing common to many big-budget fantasy movies of the past two decades. Beatty's DICK TRACY cannot be merely a movie, it must be presented as an "event"—both cultural artifact and work of art. Of course, this line of reasoning also dictates that Beatty cannot take the material seriously, and the results are faintly (but very definitely) condescending to the source. An inevitably diffused, ineffectual film, DICK TRACY was only a middling financial success, falling considerably short of box-office expectations.

DOCTOR STRANGE
comic book
Marvel Comics

DOCTOR STRANGE (CBS, 1978)—TV movie; 90 minutes; color.

Credits: Executive Producer: Phillip DeGuere; Producer: Alex Beaton; Director: Phillip Deguere; Screenplay: Philip DeGuere; Camera: Enzo A. Martinelli; Art Director: William Tunkle; Music: Paul Chihara.

Cast: Peter Hooten (Dr. Stephen Strange); Clyde Kusatsu (Wong); Jessica Walter (Morgan Le Fay); Philip Sterling (Dr. Frank Taylor); David Hooks (The Nameless One); Michael Ansara (Voice of The Ancient One); John Mills (Thomas Lindmer); Eddie Benton (Clea Lake); June Barrett (Sarah); Diane Webster (Head Nurse); Harry Anderson (Magician); Michael Clark (Taxi Driver); Bob Delegall (Intern).

Created by writer-editor Stan Lee and artist Steve Ditko, this magical superhero-adventure strip premiered in STRANGE TALES #110 in July of 1963. The book was retitled DOCTOR STRANGE with issue #169 in June of 1968.

The made-for-TV movie adaptation, although showing more attention to detail and deference to the source material than most similar productions, and benefitting from the presence of Jessica Walter as an evil sorceress, was ineffectual, in spite of the flamboyant material.

Burdened with more than its fair share of mystical pretension, this strip was more interesting for its visual rather than conceptual elements, with the magician hero owing a good deal to MANDRAKE, THE MAGICIAN.

DON WINSLOW
newspaper strip

DON WINSLOW OF THE NAVY (Universal, 1941)— theatrical serial; 12 chapters, approximately 20 minutes each.

Credits: Associate Producer: Henry MacRae; Directors: Ford Beebe, Ray Taylor; Screenplay: Paul Huston, Griffin Jay (Adaptation: Morgan B. Cox); Camera: William Sickner; Art Director: Robert Boyd; Supervising Editor: Saul A. Goodkind;

DON WINSLOW OF THE NAVY (Universal, 1941): Don Terry in the title role.

Editors: Alvin Todd, Louis Sackin, Joseph Gluck, Pat Kelley; Dialogue Director: Paul Huston.

Cast: Don Terry (Don Winslow); Walter Sande (Lieutenant Red Pennington); Wade Boteler (Mike Splendor); Paul Scott (Captain Fairfield); John Litel (Menlin); Peter Leeds (Chapman); Anne Nagel (Misty); Claire Dodd (Mercedes); Frank Lackteen (Koloki).

Chapter Titles: (1) The Human Torpedo; (2) Flaming Death; (3) Weapons of Horror; (4) Towering Doom; (5) Trapped in the Dungeon; (6) Menaced By Man-Eaters; (7) Bombed by the Enemy; (8) The Chamber of Doom; (9) Wings of Destruction; (10) Fighting Fathoms Deep; (11) Caught in the Caverns; (12) The Scorpion Strangled.

DON WINSLOW OF THE COAST GUARD (Universal, 1942)—theatrical serial; 13 chapters, approximately 20 minutes each.

Credits: Associate Producer: Henry MacRae; Directors: Ray Taylor, Lewis D. Collins; Screenplay: Paul Huston, George H. Plympton, Griffin Jay (Additional Dialogue: Richard Brooks); Camera: William Sickner, John W. Boyle; Art Director: Ralph DeLacy; Music: H. J. Salter; Supervising Editor: Saul A. Goodkind; Editors: Al Todd, Irving Birmbaum, Edgar Zane; Dialogue Director: Jacques Jaccard.

Cast: Don Terry (Comdr. Don Winslow); Walter Sande (Lt. Red Pennington); Elyse Knox (Mercedes Colby); Philip Ahn (Hirota); June Duprez (Tasmla); Edgar Dearing (CPO Ben Cobb); Lionel Royce (Reichter); Henry Victor (Heilrich); Charles Waggenheim (Mussanti); Nestor Paiva (The Scorpion).

Chapter Titles: (1) Trapped in the Blazing Sea; (2) Battling a U-Boat; (3) The Crash in the Clouds; (4) The Scorpion Strikes; (5) A Flaming Target; (6) Ramming the Submarine; (7) Bombed in the Ocean Depths; (8) Blackout Treachery; (9) The Torpedo Strikes; (10) Blasted from the Skies; (11) A Fight to the Death; (12) The Death Trap; (13) Capturing the Scorpion.

Approved by the U.S. Navy as a promotional device for attracting new recruits, DON WINSLOW OF THE NAVY was created by Lt. Comdr. Frank V. Martinek, and drawn by Lt. Leon A. Beroth, USN, and Carl Hammond. The strip, distributed by the Bell Syndicate, ran until it was discontinued in 1955.

DONDI
newspaper strip

DONDI (Allied Artists, 1961)—theatrical feature; 80 minutes.

Credits: Producers: Albert Zugsmith, Gus Edson; Director: Albert Zugsmith; Screenplay: Albert Zugsmith, Gus Edson; Camera: Carl Guthrie; Art Director: William Glasgow; Set Decorator: Rudy Butler; Editor: Edward Curtiss; Costumes: Roger J. Weinberg, Charles Arrico; Makeup: Stanley Campbell; Songs: "Dondi" (Music and Lyrics: Earl Shuman, Mort Garson); "Jingle Bells," "Meadow in the Sky"; Vocals: Patti Page; Musical Score: Morgan.

Cast: David Janssen (Dealey); Patti Page (Liz); Walter Winchell (Himself); Mickey Shaughnessy (Sergeant); Robert Strauss (Sammy Boy); Arnold Stang (Peewee); Louis Quinn (Dimmy); Gale Gordon (Colonel); Dick Patterson (Perky); Susan Kelley (Lt. Calhoun); John Melfi (Jo-Jo); Bonnie Scott (Gladdy); William Wellman, Jr. (Ted); Nola Thorp (Candy); Joan Staley (Sally); David Kory (Dondi).

Distributed by the Chicago Tribune-New York News Syndicate, this cloying humor strip, created by Gus Edson and Irwin Hasen first appeared in September of 1955. The feature film adapted from the strip is a wretched abomination, capturing the strip's mawkish "sentiment" all too well. There was also an unsold television pilot filmed.

E.C. COMICS
comic books
E.C. Comics

TALES FROM THE CRYPT (Cinerama, 1972)—theatrical feature; 92 minutes; color.

Credits: Producers: Milton Subotsky, Max J. Rosenberg; Director: Freddie Francis; Screenplay: Milton Subotsky; Camera: Norman Warrick, John Harris; Music: Douglas Gamley; Editor: Teddy Darvas; Art Director: Tony Curtis; Set Design: Helen Thomas; Makeup: Roy Ashton.

Cast: Ralph Richardson (Crypt Keeper); Geoffrey Bayldon (Guide); Joan Collins (Joanne Clayton); Marty Goddey (Richard Clayton); Oliver MacGreevy (Maniac); Chloe Franks (Carol Clayton); Ian Hendry (Carl Maitland); Paul Clere (Maitland's Son); Sharon Clere (Maitland's Daughter); Angie Grant (Susan); Susan Denny (Mrs. Maitland); Frank Forsyth (Tramp); Nigel Patrick (William Rogers); Patrick Magee (George Carter); Tony Wall (Attendant); Harry Locke (Cook); George Herbert (Old Blind Man); John Barrard, Carl Bernard, Ernest C. Jennings, Chris Cannon, Hugo De Vernier, Louis Manai (Blind Men); Peter Cushing (Grimsdyke); Robin Phillips (James Elliot); David Markham (Edward Elliot); Edward Evans (Mr. Ramsay); Ann Sears (Mrs. Carter); Irene Gawne (Mrs. Phelps); Kay Adrian (Mrs. Davies); Clifford Earl (Police Sergeant); Manning Wilson (Vicar); Dan Caulfield (Postman); Robert Hutton (Mr. Baker); Melinda Clancy (Miss Carter); Stafford Medhurst (Mrs. Phelps' Son); Carlos baker (Mrs.

Davies' Son); Richard Greene (Ralph Jason); Roy Dotrice (Charles Gregory); Barbara Murray (Enid Jason); Peter Thomas (Pallbearer); Hedger Wallace (Detective).

THE VAULT OF HORROR (Cinerama, 1973)—theatrical feature; 87 minutes; color.

Credits: Producers: Max J. Rosenberg, Milton Subotsky; Director: Roy Ward Baker; Screenplay: Milton Subotsky; Camera: Denys Coop; Music: Douglas Gamley; Editor: Oswald Hafenrichter; Art Director: Tony Curtis; Makeup: Roy Ashton.

Cast: Daniel Massey (Rogers); Anna Massey (Donna); Mike Pratt (Clive); Erik Chitty (Old Waiter); Frank Forsyth, Jerold Wells (Waiters); Michael Craig (Maitland); Edward Judd (Alex); Robin Nedwell (Tom); Geoffrey Davies (Jerry); Arthur Mullard (Gravedigger); Curt Jergens (Sebastian); Dawn Addams (Inez); Jasmine Hilton (Indian Girl); Ishaq Bux (Fakir); Terry-Thomas (Critchit); Glynis Johns (Eleanor); Marianne Stone (Jane); John Forbes-Robertson (Wilson); Tom Baker (Moore); Denholm Elliott (Diltant); Terence Alexander (Breedley); John Witty (Gaskill).

Note: This film was rereleased as TALES FROM THE CRYPT II.

TALES FROM THE CRYPT (HBO, 1989)—TV series; each episode 30 minutes; color.

Credits: Producer: Joel Silver; Directors: Roger Zemeckis, Richard Donner, Walter Hill; Writers: Fred Dekker, Terry Black, Robert Reneau; Special Effects: Kevin Yagher.

Cast: Mary Ellen Trainor; Joe Pantoliano; Robert Wuhl; Bill Sadler.

Publisher William M. Gaines inherited the family business from his father Max C. Gaines, and began his controversial line of E.C. COMICS (the "E.C." originally stood for "Educational Comics," and finally for the more apt "Entertaining Comics") in 1950. The E.C. line, which included the titles TALES FROM THE CRYPT (originally CRYPT OF TERROR), THE VAULT OF HORROR, THE HAUNT OF FEAR, WEIRD SCIENCE, WEIRD FANTASY, CRIME SUSPENSTORIES and TWO-FISTED TALES, endured for only five years, ending publication in 1955 amidst a storm of controversy and threatened censorship brought about by the graphic violence in the books and the somewhat hysterical objections of PTA groups and educators, who were spurred on in their moralistic fervor by the publication of psychiatrist Fredric M. Wertham's book *Seduction of the Innocent.* The Wertham tome was a general diatribe against the comic-book medium and its allegedly harmful effects upon impressionable youth, and the result for the comic-book industry was devastating, ushering in decades of stifling censorship. The root of the problem may have been not the graphic violence in comics, but simply the fact that they were not quite bland enough to endure in 1950s America. Nevertheless, the E.C. horror comics lived on in the memories of those who read them, and were eventually revived in reprint form. These comics have not translated well to movies, perhaps because a primary reason for their original impact was the artwork, highly detailed and often painstakingly grisly, a graphic element that cannot be duplicated on film, no matter how elaborate the special effects.

ELLA CINDERS
newspaper strip

ELLA CINDERS (First-National, 1926)—theatrical feature; 7 reels.

Credits: Producer: John McCormick; Director: Alfred E. Green; Screenplay: Frank Griffin, Mervyn Le Roy; Titles:

George Marion, Jr.; Camera: Arthur Martinelli; Editor: Robert J. Kern; Art Director: E. J. Shutter.

Cast: Colleen Moore (Ella Cinders); Lloyd Hughes (Waite Lifter); Vera Lewis (Ma Cinders); Doria Baker (Lotta Pill); Emily Gerdes (Prissy Pill); Mike Donlin (Studio Gateman); Jed Prouty (The Mayor); Jack Duffy (The Fire Chief); Harry Allen (The Photographer); D'Arcy Corrigan (The Editor); Alfred E. Green (The Director); Harry Langdon; E. H. Calvert; Chief Yowlache; Russell Hopton.

Premiering in June of 1925, this humor strip, created by Bill Counselman and Charlie Plumb, was originally distributed by the Metropolitan Newspaper Syndicate and later moved to the United Features Syndicate, until it was discontinued in the 1950s. The film version, starring Colleen Moore, is one of that charming silent star's best and most fondly remembered efforts.

THE FLASH
comic book

THE FLASH (CBS, 1990)—TV series; each episode 60 minutes; color.

Credits: Executive Producers: Danny Bilson, Paul De Meo; Executive Story Consultants: Howard Chaykin, John Francis Moore; Music: Danny Elfman; Theme Music: Shirley Walker; Flash Suit Designer: Robert Short; Costume Supervisor: Perry Kimono; Visual Effects Supervision: David Stipes, Robert Bailey.

Cast: John Wesley Shipp (Barry Allen/The Flash); Amanda Pays; Alex Desert.

Literally "the fastest man alive," The Flash first appeared in a January 1940 comic book and was created in committee by publisher Max C. Gaines and others. In reality research scientist Jay Garrick, The Flash acquired his tremendous speed as the dubious result of breathing heavy water fumes. The book was discontinued after a few years only to be reincarnated by DC Comics editor Julius Schwartz and artist Carmine Infantino in Spetember of 1956. In this later version, The Flash was police chemist Barry Allen, and was endowed with super-speed after a stray lightning bolt destroyed Allen's laboratory, exposing him to an unspecified mixture of volatile chemicals. In the wake of Warner Bros.' successful 1989 BATMAN feature (q.v.), a live action network-TV series was produced by CBS, which, although well made, was flawed by its unnecessary imitation of Warners' BATMAN, even to the extent of using theme music composed by Danny Elfman.

FLASH GORDON
newspaper strip

FLASH GORDON (Universal, 1936)—theatrical serial; 13 chapters, approximately 20 minutes each.

Credits: Producer: Henry MacRae; Directors: Frederick Stephani and (uncredited) Ray Taylor; Screenplay: Frederick Stephani, George Plympton, Basil Dickey, Ella O'Neill; Camera: Jerome H. Ash, Richard Fryer; Art Director: Ralph Berger; Electrical Effects: Norman Dewes; Electrical Properties: Kenneth Strickfaden, Raymond Lindsay; Special Properties: Elmer A. Johnson; Editors: Saul A. Goodkind, Edward Todd, Alvin Todd, Louis Sackin; Original Music: Clifford Vaughan, David Claxton; Music Supervision: Jacques Aubran; Sound: Western Electric.

FLASH GORDON (Universal, 1936): Buster Crabbe in the title role.

FLASH GORDON (Universal, 1936): An underclad Jean Rogers bulges her eyes in reaction to an off-screen menace.

Cast: Larry "Buster" Crabbe (Flash Gordon); Jean Rogers (Dale Arden); Charles Middleton (Emperor Ming); Priscilla Lawson (Princess Aura); Frank Shannon (Dr. Zarkov); Richard Alexander (Prince Barin); John Lipson (King Vultan); Theodore Lorch, Lon Poff (High Priest); James Pierce (Prince Thun); Earl Askam (Officer Torch); Duke York, Jr. (King Kala); Muriel Goodspeed (Zona); Richard Tucker (Gordon, Sr.); George Cleveland (Professor Hensley); Carroll Borland; Lynton Brent; Don Brodie; Bull Montana; Constantine Romanoff; Sana Raya; House Peters, Jr.; Jim Corey; Ray "Crash" Corrigan; Glenn Strange; Lane Chandler; Fred Kohler, Jr.; Al Ferguson; Charles Whitaker; Bunny Waters; Fred Sommers; Monte Montague; Howard Christie; Fred Scott; Jerry Frank; Bob Kortman.

Chapter Titles: (1) Planet of Peril; (2) The Tunnel of Terror; (3) Captured by Shark Men; (4) Battling the Sea Beast; (5) The Destroying Ray; (6) Flaming Torture; (7) Shattering Doom; (8) Tournament of Death; (9) Fighting the Fire Dragon; (10) The Unseen Peril; (11) In the Claws of the Tigron; (12) Trapped in the Turret; (13) Rocketing to Earth.

Note: Two different feature-length versions have been re-edited from this serial: ROCKET SHIP, for theatrical distribution, and SPACESHIP TO THE UNKNOWN, for TV syndication.

FLASH GORDON'S TRIP TO MARS (Universal, 1938)—theatrical serial; 15 chapters, approximately 20 minutes each.

Credits: Associate Producer: Barney Sarecky; Directors: Ford Beebe, Robert F. Hill; Screenplay: Wyndham Gittens, Norman S. Hall, Ray Trampe, Herbert Dalmus; Camera: Jerome H. Ash; Art Director: Ralph Delacy; Editors: Saul A. Goodkind, Alvin Todd, Louis Sackin, Joe Gluck; Dialogue Director: Sarah

FLASH GORDON'S TRIP TO MARS (Universal, 1938): C. Montague Shaw, Jean Rogers, and Buster Crabbe.

FLASH GORDON'S TRIP TO MARS (Universal, 1938): Charles Middleton as Ming the Merciless.

C. Haney; Mechanical Effects: Eddie Keys; Electrical Properties: Kenneth Strickfaden; Sound: Western Electric.

Cast: Larry "Buster" Crabbe (Flash Gordon); Jean Rogers (Dale Arden); Charles Middleton (Ming the Merciless); Beatrice Roberts (Queen Azura); Frank Shannon (Dr. Zarkov); Donald Kerr ("Happy" Hapgood); C. Montague Shaw (Clay King); Richard Alexander (Prince Barin); Wheeler Oakman (Tarnak); Kane Richmond (Stratosled Captain); Kenneth Duncan (Airdrome Captain); Warner Richmond (Zandar); Jack Mulhall (Flight Commander); Anthony Warde (Mighty Toran); Ben Lewis (Pilot); Stanley Price; Earl Douglas; Charles "Bud" Wolfe; Edwin Stanley; Lou Merrill; James C. Eagles; Hooper Atchley; James G. Blaine; Wheaton Chambers; Ray Turner; Edwin Parker; Jerry Frank; Herb Holcombe; Lane Chandler; Reed Howes; Jerry Gardner; Tom Steele; George de Normand.

Chapter Titles: (1) New Worlds to Conquer; (2) The Living Dead; (3) Queen of Magic; (4) Ancient Enemies; (5) The Boomerang; (6) Tree Men of Mars; (7) The Prisoner of Mongo; (8) The Black Sapphire of Kalu; (9) Symbol of Death; (10) Incense of Forgetfulness; (11) Human Bait; (12) Ming the Merciless; (13) The Miracle of Magic; (14) A Beast at Bay; (15) An Eye For An Eye.

Note: The release prints of this serial were tinted green. Two different feature-length versions have been re-edited from this serial: MARS ATTACKS THE WORLD, for theatrical distribution, and THE DEADLY RAY FROM MARS, for TV syndication.

FLASH GORDON CONQUERS THE UNIVERSE (Universal, 1940)—theatrical serial; 12 chapters, approximately 20 minutes each.

Credits: Associate Producer: Henry MacRae; Directors: Ford Beebe, Ray Taylor; Screenplay: George Plympton, Basil

FLASH GORDON CONQUERS THE UNIVERSE (Universal, 1940): Carol Hughes, Buster Crabbe.

FLASH GORDON CONQUERS THE UNIVERSE (Universal, 1940): Buster Crabbe, Lee Powell, Anne Gwynne, Carol Hughes, and Don Rowan.

FLASH GORDON CONQUERS THE UNIVERSE (Universal, 1940): Carol Hughes and Buster Crabbe.

Dickey, Barry Shipman; Camera: Jerome H. Ash, William Sickner; Art Director: Harold H. MacArthur; Dialogue Director: Jacques Jaccard; Editors: Saul A. Goodkind, Alvin Todd, Louis Sackin, Joe Gluck; Electrical Properties: Kenneth Strickfaden; Assistant Directors: Edward Tyler, Charles Gould; Sound: Western Electric.

Cast: Larry "Buster" Crabbe (Flash Gordon); Carol Hughes (Dale Arden); Charles Middleton (Emperor Ming); Anne Gwynne (Sonja); Frank Shannon (Dr. Zarkov); Lee Powell (Roka); Roland Drew (King Barin); Shirley Deane (Queen Aura); Donald Curtis (Captain Ronal); Don Rowan (Captain Torch); Sigurd Nilssen (Count Korro); Michael Mark (Karm); William Royle (Captain Sudin); Victor Zimmerman (Thong); Edgar Edwards (Turan); Tom Chatterton (Arden); Henry C. Bradley (Keedish); Mimi Taylor (Verna); Byron Foulger (Drulk); Benjamin Taggart (General Lupi); Earl Dwire (Zandar); Luli Deste (Queen Fria); Jack Roper (Giant); Charles Sherlock; Paul Reed; Harold Daniels; Edward Payson; Reed Howes; Clarice Sherry; Jack Gardner; Joey Ray; Paul Douglas; Ernie Adams; Edward Mortimer; Robert Blair; Bill Hunter; Charles Waldron, Jr.; Pat Gleason; Frank Hagney; Ray Mala; Chief Yowlatchie; John Hamilton; Herbert Rawlinson; Jeanne Kelly (Jean Brooks); Allan Cavan; John Elliott; Roy Barcroft; Carmen D'Antonio.

Chapter Titles: (1) The Purple Death; (2) Freezing Torture; (3) Walking Bombs; (4) The Destroying Ray; (5) The Palace of Terror; (6) Flaming Death; (7) The Land of the Dead; (8) The Fiery Abyss; (9) The Pool of Death; (10) The Death Mist; (11) Stark Treachery; (12) Doom of the Dictator.

Note: Two different feature-length versions have been re-edited from this serial, both for TV syndication: THE PURPLE DEATH FROM OUTER SPACE and PERILS FROM THE PLANET MONGO.

FLASH GORDON (Syndicated, 1953)—TV series; 39 episodes, 30 minutes each.

Credits: Producer: Wenzel Luedecke; Director: Wallace Worsle, Jr.; Series Writers: Earl Markham, Bruce Elliot; Music: Kurt Heuser.

Cast: Steve Holland (Flash Gordon); Irene Champion (Dale Arden); Joseph Naish (Dr. Alexis Zarkov).

FLASH GORDON (Universal, 1980)—theatrical feature; 110 minutes; color.

Credits: Producer: Dino De Laurentiis; Director: Mike Hodges; Screenplay: Lorenzo Semple, Jr., Michael Allin; Camera: Gil Taylor (Todd-AO, Technicolor); Music: Howard Blake; Editor: Malcolm Cooke; Production Design: Danilo Donati; Art Direction: John Graysmark; Set Decorations: Danilo Donati; Costumes: Danilo Donati; Special Effects: George Gibbs, Richard Conway (models and skies), Derek Botel (flying scenes).

Cast: Sam J. Jones (Flash Gordon); Melody Anderson (Dale Arden); Topol (Dr. Hans Zarkov); Max Von Sydow (Emperor Ming); Ornella Muti (Princess Aura); Timothy Dalton (Prince Barin); Brian Blessed (Prince Vultan); Peter Wyngarde (Klytus); Mariangelo Melato (Kala); John Osborne (Arborian Priest); Richard O'Brien (Fico); John Hallam (Luro); Philip Stone (Zogi, the High Priest); Suzanne Danielle (Serving Girl); William Hootkins (Munson); Bobbie Brown (Hedonia); Ted Carroll (Biro); Adrienne Kronenberg (Vultan's Daughter); Stanley Lebor (Mongon Doctor); John Morton, Burnell Tucker (Airline Pilots); Robbie Coltrane (Man at Airport); Peter Duncan (Young Treeman); Ken Sicklen (Treeman); Tessa, Vanetia Spicer (Hawkwomen); Francis Mugham (Wounded Hawkman); Paul Bentall (Klytus' Pilot); Oliver Mac Greevy (Klytus' Observer #1); John Hollis (Klytus' Observer #2); Tony Scannell (Ming's Officer); Leon Greene (Colonel in Battle Control Room); Graeme Crowther (Battle Room Controller); David Neal (Captain of Ming's Air Force); Deep Roy (Princess Aura's Pet); Sally Nicholson (Queen of Azuria); Doretta Dunkler (Queen of Frigia); Colin Taylor (King of Frigia); George Harris (Prince of Ardentia); Miranda Riley (Frigian Girl); Andrew Bradford, Bertram Adams, Terry Forrestal, Mike Potter, John Sullivan, John Lees, Eddie Stacy, Ray Scammell (Hawkmen); Robert Goody, Peter S. James, Steven Payne, Daniel Venn, Max Alford, Anthony Oliver, Stephen Calcutt, Stuart Blake, Nigel Jeffcoat, Jim Carter (Azurdian Men); Trevor Warde, Alva Shelley, Joe Iles, Nik Abraham, Glen Whittier, Leonard Hay (Ardentian Men); Jamalia, Sunanka, Jil Lamb, Karen Johnson (Ming's Serving Girls); Kathy Marquis, Kathy September, Sophie, Glenna Forster Jones (Sandmoon Girls); Rosanne Romine, Sneh, Shaka, Magda, Linda, Viva, Camella, Frances Ward, Beverly Andrews, Kerry Loy Baylis (Cytherian Girls); Lorraine Paul, Carolyn Evans, Ruthie Barnett, Celeste, Tina Thomas (Acquarian Girls); Racquel, Fai, Gina (Ming's Exotic Girls); Eddie Powell, Chris Webb, John Gallant, Les Crawford, Peter Brace, Terry Richards (Ming's Brutes); Kenny Baker, Malcolm Dixon, Mike Edmonds, Tiny Ross, John Ghavan, Rusty Goffe, Mike Cottrell, Peter Burrows, Richard Jones, John Lummis (Dwarfs); Michael Mildwater, Marie Green, Imogen Claire, Kay Zimmerman, Stephen Brigden, Ken Robertson, Fred Warder, Lionel Guyett.

Created by Alex Raymond, the first installment of FLASH GORDON appeared in January of 1934, distributed by King Features Syndicate.

Although initially created as an imitation of BUCK ROGERS, Raymond's strip had more textured characters, more finely developed plots and far deeper romantic and sexual implications, and soon eclipsed BUCK ROGERS in appeal and popularity.

Both the strip and the three Universal Pictures serials adapted from it have a deep mythic appeal that is very satisfying; the serials, in spite of (or perhaps because of) their frequent crudeness and cheapness, have a romantic texture and retain an emotional impact that the bigger-budgeted STAR WARS films of recent years (and the spoofy 1980 "remake" of FLASH GORDON) somehow lack.

Of the three serials, the original is by far the best, with the tightest plot and most believable characterizations. FLASH GORDON was filmed in late 1935, and derives a great deal of its effectiveness from a vintage feel that the two sequels lack. This cliffhanger was perfectly cast, with Buster Crabbe, Charles Middleton, Jean Rogers, Priscilla Lawson, Frank Shannon, and Richard Alexander all quite effective in their roles. One of the few sexually aware serials (the four-way romance involving Flash, Dale, Ming, and Aura is established immediately in the opening chapter and exploited throughout), FLASH GORDON may well be the only serial to have been censored for partial nudity. Jean Rogers recently informed this writer that when scenes of Priscilla Lawson filmed for chapter one revealed a bit too much of Lawson's ample bosom, the censors deemed the shots unacceptable and ordered them reshot—with Lawson (who essayed her "bad girl" role with what George Turner, writing in an *American Cinematographer* article on the serials, termed "undisguised carnality") wearing slightly more restraining garb. Perhaps because of the female pulchritude on display as much as any other quality, FLASH GORDON was one of the most successful and widely seen serials ever made, playing evening performances in first-run theaters and running for decades on television in later years.

The first sequel, FLASH GORDON'S TRIP TO MARS, is cheaper than the original and a bit choppy editorially; some of the scenes were so hastily shot that they do not match. Although all of the principals from the first serial were back in TRIP TO MARS, there was considerably less characterization than in FLASH GORDON, and there was not even a hint of the sexual undercurrent that made the original so compelling. Jean Rogers, whose underclad blonde's good looks made her so fetching in the first serial, sported shortened brunette hair in the sequel, not to mention considerably more clothing, and looked like a different actress altogether—especially in juxtaposition with the many clips from the first serial that were edited into the new film as padding. Charles Middleton, whose enjoyably theatrical Ming nearly stole the show in FLASH GORDON, was forced to share the villainous spotlight with Beatrice Roberts as the Martian Azura, Queen of Magic, in FLASH GORDON'S TRIP TO MARS. Although Roberts' performance is sincere and competent, she is somewhat miscast, lacking the exotic appeal necessary for such a role, and the same is true of Wheeler Oakman (a veteran "B" western heavy) as Tarnak, Ming's assistant. Comic actor Donald Kerr's slapstick performance as bumbling "comic relief" reporter Happy Hapgood was an irritation to many viewers, too, but despite flaws, FLASH GORDON'S TRIP TO MARS is still a lot of fun, and contains some of the most fondly remembered gimmicks and characters of the series, such as the Clay People.

The third entry in the series, FLASH GORDON CON-QUERS THE UNIVERSE, is the slickest of the trio, boasting glistening photography, elaborate art direction, and a stirring musical score that incorporates stock Universal Pictures musi-cal themes as well as classical compositions such as Franz Liszt's *Les Préludes*. In this serial, lovely Carol Hughes replaced Jean Rogers as Dale, and different actors were cast in the roles of Aura and Barin as well. Although it is, in many ways, the most carefully produced entry in the trilogy, FLASH GORDON CONQUERS THE UNIVERSE, for all its impressive slickness (and in the impoverished realm of serials, it is *very* impressive), still lacks the depth and appeal of the original FLASH GORDON. Of his stint as Flash in these serials, Buster Crabbe told this writer in 1981:

> To bring it [the first serial] in on the six-week schedule, we had to average eight-five set-ups a day; that means moving and rearranging the heavy equipment we had, the arc lights and everything, eighty-five times a day. We had to be in makeup every morning at 7:00, and on the set at 8:00 ready to go. They'd knock off for lunch, and then we always worked after dinner; they'd give us a break of a half-hour or forty-five minutes and then we'd go back to the set and work until 10:30 every night. It wasn't fun, it was a lot of *work!*

Today's shooting schedules are luxurious by comparison, and the fact that Crabbe and his co-workers were able to create something so memorable under such restrictive conditions (the total budget for the entire thirteen chapters of the first serial was a reported $350,000) is evidence of their genuine skill and talent.

FRIDAY FOSTER
newspaper strip

FRIDAY FOSTER (American-International Pictures, 1975)—theatrical feature; 89 minutes; color.

Credits: Producer and Director: Arthur Marks; Screenplay: Orville Hampton (Original Story: Arthur Marks); Camera: Harry May; Music: Luchi De Jesus; Music and Lyrics: Bodie Chandler; Editor: Stanley Frazen; Stunts: Richard Geary.

Cast: Pam Grier (Friday Foster); Yaphet Kotto (Colt Hawkins); Godfrey Cambridge (Ford Malotte); Thalmus Rasulala (Blake Tarr); Eartha Kitt (Madame Rena); Jim Backus (Enos Griffith); Scatman Crothers (Rev. Noble Franklin); Ted Lange (Fancy Dexter); Tierre Turner (Cleve); Paul Benjamin (Sen. David Lee Hart).

FRIDAY FOSTER, distributed by the Chicago Tribune-New York News Syndicate, premiered in January of 1970. The strip was written by Jim Lawrence and drawn by Jorge Longaren. The heroine, a glamorous black photographer, often found herself enmeshed in adventurous situations that (as timidly as possible) dealt with the racial tensions of the day. As the fashionable social consciousness of the 1960s and 1970s faded, FRIDAY FOSTER lost popularity, and was finally discontinued in 1974.

GASOLINE ALLEY
newspaper strip

GASOLINE ALLEY (Columbia, 1951)—theatrical feature; 76 minutes.

Credits: Producer: Milton Feldman; Director: Edward Bernds; Screenplay: Edward Bernds; Camera: Lester White; Editor: Aaron Stell; Music: Mischa Bakaleinikoff; Art Director: Victor Green.

Cast: Scotty Beckett (Corky); Jimmy Lydon (Skeezix); Susan Morrow (Hope); Don Beddoe (Walt Wallet); Pattie Brady (Judy); Madelon Mitchell (Phyllis); Dick Wessel (Pudge); Gus Schilling (Joe Allen); Kay Christopher (Nina); Byron Foulger (Charles D. Haven); Virginia Toland (Carol Rice); Jimmy Lloyd (Harry Dorsey); William Forrest (Hacker); Ralph Peters (Reddick); Charles Halton (Pettit); Charles Williams (Mortie); Christine McIntyre (Myrtle).

CORKY OF GASOLINE ALLEY (Columbia, 1951)— theatrical feature; 80 minutes.

Credits: Producer: Wallace MacDonald; Director: Edward Bernds; Screenplay: Edward Bernds; Camera: Henry Freulich; Editor: Jerome Thomas; Music: Mischa Bakaleinikoff.

Cast: Scotty Beckett (Corky); Jimmy Lydon (Skeezix); Don Beddoe (Walt Wallet); Gordon Jones (Elwood Martin); Patti Brady (Judy); Susan Morrow (Hope); Kay Christopher (Nina); Madelon Mitchell (Phyllis); Dick Wessel (Pudge McKay); Harry Tyler (Avery); Ralph Votrian (Larry); John Doucette (Rocky); Clarence Williams (Morde); Lester Matthews (Ellis); Jack Rice (Ames); Ludwig Stossel (Dr. Hammerschlag); John Dehner (Jefferson Jay); Lewis Russel (Hull).

GASOLINE ALLEY premiered in November of 1918. Created by Frank King, this long-running humor strip was distributed by the Chicago Tribune-New York News Syndicate.

When negotiations with King Features for the rights to produce further BLONDIE movies ended in failure, Columbia Pictures decided to produce a GASOLINE ALLEY series instead, with less-than-satisfying results. After only two entries, the proposed series was discontinued.

THE GUMPS
newspaper strip

THE GUMPS (Universal, 1923–28)—theatrical short subjects; 2 reels, approximately 20 minutes each.

Credits: Producer (Numbers 1–12): Sam Von Ronkel; Directors: Erle C. Kenton, Ray Gray, William Watson, Norman Taurog, David Kirkland, Craig Hutchinson, Francis Corby, Del Andrews, Norman Dawn, Robert Kerr, Vin Moore; Screenplays: Phil Dunham, Melville Brown, Dick Smith, Norman Taurog, Marks and Pagano, Vin Moore, Robert Kerr, William Weber; Continuity: Victor Potbel, Kerry Clark.

Titles: *1923/25:* UNCLE BIM'S GIFT; WATCH PAPA; OH, WHAT A DAY; AGGRAVATIN' MAMA; OH, MIN; WHAT'S THE USE?; ANDY'S TEMPTATION; A DAY OF REST; WESTBOUND; ANDY'S HAT IN THE RING; ANDY'S STUMP SPEECH; ANDY IN HOLLYWOOD; *1925/26:* ANDY'S LION TALE; CHESTER'S DONKEY PARTY; DYNAMITED; ANDY TAKES A FLIER; THE SMASH-UP; MIN'S HOME ON THE CLIFF; MIN WALKS IN HER SLEEP; CALIFORNIA, HERE WE COME; SHADY REST; MIN'S

AWAY; DUMB LUCK; TOW SERVICE; *1926/27:* NEVER AGAIN; LOTS OF GRIEF; BETTER LUCK; THE BIG SURPRISE; A CLOSE CALL; I TOLD YOU SO; ROOMS FOR RENT; UP AGAINST IT; YOUTH AND BEAUTY; BROKE AGAIN; I'M THE SHERIFF; CIRCUS DAZE; *1927/28:* TOO MUCH SLEEP; A BATTLE SCARED HERO; WHEN GREEK MEETS GREEK; AND HOW; OCEAN BRUISES; TOTAL LOSS; ANDY NOSE HIS ONIONS; THE MILD WEST; A CASE OF SCOTCH; ANY OLD COUNT; THE CLOUD BUSTER; OUT IN THE RAIN.

Created by Sidney Smith for the *Chicago Tribune,* THE GUMPS was a domestic-humor strip, featuring a supposedly typical lower-middle-class family comprised of Andy Gump, his wife Minerva (Min), their son Chester, their pet cat Hope, and their dog Buck. Smith had been assigned to the strip by *Tribune* publisher Joseph Patterson, and the feature initially appeared on February 12, 1917. The strip achieved wide popularity, but when Sidney Smith tragically died in a 1935 car accident, replacement artist Gus Edson failed to maintain Smith's level of humor and quality. The strip limped along, gradually declining in popularity, until it was discontinued in 1959. In the 1920s, Universal Pictures released a series of live-action comedies based on the strip.

HAIRBREADTH HARRY
newspaper strip

Created by C. W. Kahles for the Philadelphia Ledger Syndicate in 1906, this humor-adventure strip ran until it was discontinued in 1939. Six two-reel comedies based on the strip were produced in 1925 by the West brothers for their Happiness Comedies series distributed by Artclass Pictures.

HAROLD TEEN
newspaper strip

HAROLD TEEN (First-National, 1928)—theatrical feature; 8 reels.

Credits: Producer: Allan Dwan; Director: Mervyn Le Roy; Screenplay and Titles: Tom J. Geraghty; Camera: Ernest Haller; Editor: Le Roy Stone.

Cast: Arthur Lake (Harold Teen); Mary Brian (Lillums Lovewell); Lucien Littlefield (Dad Jenks); Jack Duffy (Grandpop Teen); Alice White (Giggles Dewberry); Jack Egan (Horace Teen); Hedda Hopper (Mrs. Hazzit); Ben Hall (Goofy); William Bakewell (Percival); Lincoln Stedman (Beezie); Fred Kelsey (Mr. Lovewell); Jane Keckley (Mrs. Teen); Ed Brady (Officer Axel Dewberry); Virginia Sale (Mrs. Schmittenberger).

HAROLD TEEN (Warner Bros., 1934)—theatrical feature; 67 minutes (*GB:* THE DANCING FOOL).

Credits: Director: Murray Roth; Screenplay: Paul G. Smith, Al Cohn; Camera: Arthur Todd; Art Director: John Hughes; Musical Director: Leo F. Forbstein; Music and Lyrics: Irving Kahal, Sammy Fain; Musical Numbers: "How Do You Know It's Sunday?"; "Simple and Sweet"; "Two Little Flies on a Lump of Sugar"; "Collegiate Wedding."

Cast: Hal Le Roy (Harold); Rochelle Hudson (Lillums); Patricia Ellis (Mimi); Guy Kibbee (Pa Lovewell); Hugh Herbert (Rathburn); Hobart Cavanaugh (Pop); Chic Chandler (Lilacs); Eddie Tamblyn (Shadow); Douglas Dumbrille (Snatcher); Clara Blandick (Ma Lovewell); Mayo Methot; Richard Carle; Charles Wilson.

THE LOVE LIFE OF HAROLD TEEN, later retitled simply HAROLD TEEN, first appeared in May of 1919, created by the *Chicago Tribune's* co-publisher Joseph Patterson and drawn by Carl Ed. The strip was distributed by the Chicago Tribune-New York News Syndicate until it was discontinued in 1959.

HAZEL
magazine cartoon

HAZEL (NBC, CBS, 1961–66)—TV series; 154 episodes, 30 minutes each; color.

Credits: Executive Producer: Harry Ackerman; Producer: James Fonda; Series Directors: William D. Russell, Charles Barton, E. W. Swackhamer, Hal Cooper; Series Writers: William Cowley, Peggy Chantler, Robert Riley Crutcher, Ted Sherdeman, Jane Klove, Louella MacFarland, John Mc-Greevey; Creators: William Cowley, Peggy Chantler; Music: Van Alexander, Howard Blake, Charles Albertine, Ed Forsyth.

Cast: Shirley Booth (Hazel Burke); Don DeFore (George Baxter); Whitney Blake (Dorothy Baxter); Bobby Buntrock (Harold Baxter); Ray Fulmore (Steve Baxter); Lynn Borden (Barbara Baxter); Julia Benjamin (Susie Baxter); Maudie Prickett (Rosie Hamicker); Cathy Lewis (Deirdre Thompson); Robert P. Lieb (Harry Thompson); Davey Davison (Nancy Thompson); Howard Smith (Harvey Griffin); Molly Dodd (Miss Scott); Robert B. Williams (Barney Hatfield); Patrick McVey (Gus Jenkins); Alice Backus (Clara); Mary Scott (Miss Sharp); Norma Varden (Harriet Johnson); Donald Foster (Herbert Johnson); Johnny Washbrook (Eddie Burke); Dub Taylor (Mitch Brady); John Newton (Stan Blake); Brenda Scott (Linda Blake); Judy Erwin (Mavis Blake); Paul Engle (Don Blake);

Mala Powers (Mona Williams); Charles Bateman (Fred Williams); Pat Cardi (Jeff Williams); Ann Jillian (Millie Ballard); Lawrence Haddon (Bill Fox); Harvey Grant (Ted Drake); Dick Sargent (Mr. Griffin's Nephew).

This humor strip was created by Ted Key for *The Saturday Evening Post*. The bland TV situation-comedy adaptation, starring Shirley Booth as Key's comical maid, was mild and inoffensive, running for several unobtrusive seasons. Television viewers really didn't notice the show when it was on, and in all probability didn't miss it when it was cancelled.

HOWARD THE DUCK
comic book
Marvel Comics

HOWARD THE DUCK (Universal, 1986)—theatrical feature; 111 minutes; color.

Credits: Producer: Gloris Katz; Director: Willard Huyck; Screenplay: Willard Huyck, Gloria Katz; Camera: Richard H. Kline; Music: John Barry; Editors: Michael Chandler, Sidney Wolinski; Production Design: Peter Jamison; Art Directors: Blake Russell, Mark Billerman; Set Design: Jim Pohl, Pamela Marcotte; Costumes: Joe Tompkins; Special Effects: Bob MacDonald, Jr.; Choreography: Sarah Elgart; Music and Lyrics: Thomas Dolby, Alice Willis, George Clinton, Delbert McClinton, Frederick Lowe, Alan Jay Lerner; Makeup: Karen Bradley.

Cast: Lea Thompson (Beverly Switzler); Jeffrey Jones (Dr. Jennings); Tim Robbins (Phil Blumburtt); Ed Gale; Chip Zien; Tim Rose; Steve Sleap; Peter Baird; Mary Wells; Lisa Sturz;

Jordan Prentice (Howard T. Duck); Paul Guilfoyle (Lieutenant Welker); Liz Sagal (Ronette); Dominique Davalos (Cal); Holly Robinson (K. C.); Tommy Swerdlow (Ginger Moss); Richard Edson (Ritchie); Miles Chapin (Carter); Richard McGonagle (Cop); Virginia Capers (Coramae); Debbie Carrington (Additional Ducks); Jorli McClain (Waitress); Michael Sandoval (Club Owner); Sheldon Feldner (Hot Tub Spa Owner); Lee Anthony (Grossbach); Paul Comi (Dr. Chapin); Maureen Coyne (Teacher); James Lashley (State Trooper); Tom Parker (TV Reporter); Ed Holmes (TV Duck Hunter); David Paymer (Larry Scientist); William Hall (Hanson); Denny Delk (Sergeant); Martin Ganapoler, Tim Rayhall, Gary Littlejohn (Truckers); Thomas Dolby (Bartender); Kristopher Logan (Punk); Reed Kirk Rahlman (Bender); John Fleck; William McCoy; Steve Kravitz; Ann Tofflemire; Marcia Banks; Nancy Fish; Monty Hoffman; Ted Kurtz; Wood Moy; Wanda McCaddon; James Brady; Carol McElheney; Jeanne Lauren; Margarita Fernandez; Felix Silla; Richard Kiley.

This cynical and archly self-conscious humor-fantasy strip was premiered in ADVENTURE INTO FEAR #19 in 1973, and was quickly awarded its own book. The movie version of the strip, produced by George Lucas at a cost of millions, was one of the most notorious box-office flops in recent movie history. The strip dealt with the adventures of a talking duck transported to earth from another world, and his reactions to (as well as his ascerbic running commentary on) his alien environment.

THE HULK
comic book

THE INCREDIBLE HULK (CBS, 1977)—TV movie; 120 minutes; color.

Credits: Producer: Kenneth Johnson; Director: Kenneth Johnson; Screenplay: Kenneth Johnson; Camera: Howard Schwartz; Music: Joseph Harnell; Editors: Jack Shoengarth, Alan Marks.

Cast: Bill Bixby (Dr. David Banner); Lou Ferrigno (The Hulk); Jack Colvin (Jack McGee); Susan Sullivan (Elaine Marks); Susan Batson (Mrs. Maier); Charles Siebert (Ben); Mario Gallo (Mr. Bram); Eric Server (Policeman); Eric Deon (B. J.); Jake Mitchell (Jerry); Lara Parker (Laura Banner); William Larsen (Minister); Olivia Barash (Girl at Lake); George Brenlin (Man at Lake); June Whitley (Woman); Terrence Locke (Young Man).

THE RETURN OF THE INCREDIBLE HULK (CBS, 1977)— TV movie; 120 minutes; color.

Credits: Director: Alan Levi; Screenplay: Kenneth Johnson.

Cast: Bill Bixby (Dr. David Banner); Lou Ferrigno (The Hulk); Jack Colvin (Jack McGee); Laurie Prange (Julie Griffith); Dorothy Tristan (Margaret Griffith); Gerald McRaney (Denny); William Daniels (Dr. Bonifant).

THE INCREDIBLE HULK (CBS, 1978–82)—TV series; 87 episodes, 60 minutes each; color.

Credits: Executive Producer: Kenneth Johnson; Supervising Producer: Nicholas Corea; Producers: James D. Parriott, Chuck Bowman, Nicholas Corea, James G. Hirsch, Robert Steinhauer, Karen Harris, Jill Sherman, Andrew Schneider; Series Directors: Alan J. Levi, Kenneth G. Gilbert, Larry Stewart, Sigmund Neufeld, Jr., Jeffrey Hayden, Harvey S. Laidman, Reza S. Badiyi, Frank Orsatti, Joseph Pevney, Ray Danton, Chuck Bowman, Chuck McPherson, Barry Crane, Richard Milton,

THE INCREDIBLE HULK (CBS-TV, 1977): Lou Ferrigno and Bill Bixby.

Patrick Boyrivan, Bernard McEveety, Michael Vejar, John Liberti; Series Writers: Kenneth Johnson, Karen Harris, Jill Sherman, James D. Parriott, William Schwartz, Tom Szollosi, Richard Matheson, Justin Edgerton, Jim Tisdale, Paul M. Delous, Robert Wolterstoff, Nicholas Corea, Jaron Summers, Frank Dandridge, Joel Don Humphreys, William Whitehead, Susan Woollen, Bruce Kalish, Philip Taylor, Brian Rehak, Migdia Varels, Ben Masselink, Deborah Davis, James G. Hirsch, Craig Buck, Dan Ullman, Sam Egan, Chuck Bowman, Andrew Schneider, Len Jenkins, Alan Cole, Chris Bunch, James Parker, George Bloom, Reuben Leder, Carol Baxter, Nancy Faulkner, Alan Cassidy, Diane Frolov, Jeri Taylor; Camera: John McPherson, Charles W. Short; Art Directors: Frank Grieco, Charles R. Davis, David Marshall, Seymour Klate; Music: Joseph Harnell, Charles R. Cassey; Theme Music: Joe Harnell.

Cast: Bill Bixby (Dr. David Banner); Lou Ferrigno (The Hulk); Jack Colvin (Jack McGee); Ric Drasin (Demi Hulk); Susan Sullivan (Elaina Marks).

THE INCREDIBLE HULK RETURNS (NBC, 1988)—TV movie; 120 minutes; color.

Credits: Executive Producers: Nicholas Corea, Bill Bixby; Supervising Producer: Daniel McPhee; Director: Nicholas Corea; Screenplay: Nicholas Corea; Camera: Chuck Colwell; Music: Lance Rabin.

Cast: Bill Bixby; Lou Ferrigno; Jack Colvin; Lee Purcell; Eric Kramer; Charles Napier; John Gabriel; Jay Baker; Tim Thomerson; Steve Levitt; William Riley; Tom Finnegan; Donald Willis; Carl Nick Ciafalio; Bobby Travis McLaughlin; Burke Denis; Nick Costa; Peisha McPhee; William Malone; Joanie Allen.

THE TRIAL OF THE INCREDIBLE HULK (NBC, 1989)—
TV movie; 120 minutes; color.

Credits: Executive Producers: Bill Bixby, Gerald Dipego; Producers: Hugh Spencer-Phillips, Robert Ewing; Director: Bill Bixby; Screenplay: Gerald Dipego; Camera: Chuck Colwell; Music: Lance Rubin.

Cast: Bill Bixby; Lou Ferrigno; Mata Dubois; Nancy Everhard; Nicholas Hormann; Richard Cummings, Jr.; Joseph Mascolo; John Rhys-Davies; Rex Smith; Linda Darlow; John Novak; Dwight Koss; Meredith Woodward; Mark Acheson; Richard Newman; Don McKay; Doug Abrahams; Mitchell Kosterman; Beatrice Zeilinger; Ken Camroux; Charles Andre; John Bear Curtis.

The Hulk, created by writer-editor Stan Lee and artist Jack Kirby, was introduced in THE INCREDIBLE HULK #1 in May of 1962. The book lasted only six issues, but the character continued in TALES TO ASTONISH beginning with issue #59 in August of 1964, and the title was eventually changed to THE INCREDIBLE HULK with issue #102 in April of 1968.

The long-running TV series starring Bill Bixby and Lou Ferrigno had little to do with the original comic books beyond the basic premise, and the shows persisted in diluting the fantasy elements in favor of "human interest" stories, with the monstrous Hulk's appearances kept to an economical minimum. When the series was finally cancelled and two later made-for-TV features were produced in an attempt to revive the show, two other Marvel Comics characters, Thor and Daredevil, were represented in these films. Predictably, the adaptations of these characters were no more faithful to the comic-book source than the Bixby/Ferrigno Hulk.

JANE
newspaper strip

THE ADVENTURES OF JANE (New World/Keystone, 1949)—theatrical feature; 55 minutes.

Credits: Producer: Edward G. Whiting; Directors: Edward G. Whiting, Alf Goulding; Screenplay: Edward G. Whiting, Alf Goulding, Con West; Camera: Jack Rose.

Cast: Christabel Leighton-Porter (Jane); Stanelli (Hotelier); Michael Hogarth (Tom Hawke); Wally Patch (Customs Officer); Ian Cohn (Captain Cleaver); Sonya O'Shea (Ruby); Peter Butterworth (Drunk); Sebastian Cabot (Traveler).

JANE AND THE LOST CITY (New World, 1987)—theatrical feature; 93 minutes; color.

Credits: Producer: Harry Robertson; Director: Terry Marcel; Screenplay: Mervyn Haisman; Camera: Paul Beeson; Editor: Alan Jones; Music: Harry Robertson; Designer: Mick Pickwoad; Sound: Alan Gerhardt; Assistant Director: Graham Hickson.

Cast: Kirsten Hughes (Jane); Sam Jones (Jungle Jack Buck); Maud Adams (Lola Pagola); Jasper Carrott (Heinrich); Robin Bailey (Colonel); Jan Roberts (Carl); Elsa O'Toole (Leopard Queen); Graham Stark; John Rapley.

Created by Norman Pett, JANE is one of Great Britain's most famous comic strips, and for good reason. The attractive heroine was inclined to strip her clothes off. Frequently. The strip began in December of 1932, appearing in the *Daily Mirror*, with Pett's shapely wife posing for the drawings of Jane, although other models were also used. Understandably, JANE was a huge success with servicemen, and during World War II a model, Christabel Leighton-Porter, played the character in a strip-tease act that toured British music halls. Leighton-Porter also played Jane in the 1949 feature film. Jane herself left Pett's strip in 1959, and, the vitality gone, the strip limped along featuring supporting characters until it was discontinued in 1963.

JOE PALOOKA
newspaper strip

PALOOKA (Reliance–United Artists, 1934)—theatrical feature; 86 minutes (a.k.a. JOE PALOOKA; GB: THE GREAT SCHNOZZOLA).

Credits: Director: Benjamin Stoloff; Screenplay: Ben Ryan, Murray Roth, Jack Jevne, Arthur Kober; Camera: Arthur Edeson; Editor: Grant Whytlock; Songs: Jimmy Durante, Ben Ryan ("Ink-a-Dinka-Do"), Harold Adamson, Burton Lane ("Like Me a Little Bit Less, Love Me a Little Bit More"), Ann Ronnell, Joe Burke ("Palooka, It's a Grand Old Name"), Irving Caesar, Ferde Grofe, Edgar A. Guest ("Count Your Blessings").

Cast: Jimmy Durante (Knobby Walsh); Lupe Velez (Nina Madero); Stuart Erwin (Joe Palooka); Marjorie Rambeau (Mayme Palooka); Robert Armstrong (Pete Palooka); Mary Carlisle (Anne); William Cagney (Al McSwatt); Thelma Todd (Trixie); Franklyn Ardel (Doc Wise); Tom Dugan (Whitey); Guinn "Big Boy" Williams (Slats); Stanley Fields (Blacky); Louise Beavers (Crystal); Fred "Snowflake" Toomes (Smokey); Gordon De Main (Photographer's Official); Gus Arnheim and his Orchestra.

THE BLONDE BOMBER (Vitaphone, 1936)—theatrical short subject; 20 minutes.

Credits: Director: Lloyd French; Screenplay: Jack Henley, A. Dorian Otvos, Eddie Forman.

Cast: Robert Norton; Shemp Howard; Lee Weber; Harry Gribbon; Johnny Berkes; Mary Doran.

FOR THE LOVE OF PETE (Vitaphone, 1936)—theatrical short subject; 21 minutes.

Credits: Director: Lloyd French; Screenplay: Jack Henley, Burnet Hershey.

Cast: Robert Norton; Shemp Howard; Lucy Parker; Johnny Berkes; Richard Lane; Michael Dennis; Charlie Althoss; Buddy Bueler; Rex.

HERE'S HOWE (Vitaphone, 1936)—theatrical short subject; 21 minutes.

Credits: Director: Lloyd French; Screenplay: Jack Henley, Burnet Hershey, Robert Mako.

Cast: Robert Norton; Shemp Howard; Leo Webberman; Beverly Phalon.

PUNCH AND BEAUTY (Vitaphone, 1936)—theatrical short subject; 20 minutes (*a.k.a.* THE CHOKE'S ON YOU).

Credits: Director: Lloyd French; Screenplay: Jack Henley, Burnet Hershey, Eddie Forman.

Cast: Robert Norton; Shemp Howard; Beverly Phalon; Johnny Berkes.

CALLING ALL KIDS (Vitaphone, 1937)—theatrical short subject; 17 minutes.

Credits: Director: Lloyd French; Screenplay: Jack Henley, Eddie Forman.

Cast: Robert Norton; Beverly Phalon; Johnny Berkes.

KICK ME AGAIN (Vitaphone, 1937)—theatrical short subject; 21 minutes.

Credits: Director: Lloyd French; Screenplay: Jack Henley, Eddie Forman.

Cast: Robert Norton; Shemp Howard; Beverly Phalon; Lee Weber.

TAKING THE COUNT (Vitaphone, 1937)—theatrical short subject; 21 minutes.

Credits: Director: Lloyd French; Screenplay: Jack Henley, Eddie Forman.

Cast: Robert Norton; Shemp Howard; Beverly Phalon; Charles Kemper; Johnny Berkes; Regina Wallace; John Vosbough; Jack Shutta.

THIRST AID (Vitaphone, 1937)—theatrical short subject; 20 minutes.

Cast: Robert Norton; Beverly Phalon.

GENTLEMAN JOE PALOOKA (Monogram, 1946)—theatrical feature; 72 minutes.

GENTLEMAN JOE PALOOKA (Monogram, 1946): An original theatre poster.

Credits: Producer: Hal E. Chester; Director: Cyril Endfield; Screenplay: Cyril Endfield.

Cast: Leon Errol; Joe Kirkwood, Jr.; Elyse Knox; Guy Kibbee; Lionel Stander; H. B. Warner; Stanley Prager; Richard Lane; Warren Hymer; Cliff Nazarro; Fritz Feld.

JOE PALOOKA, CHAMP (Monogram, 1946)—theatrical feature; 70 minutes.

Credits: Producer: Hal E. Chester; Director: Reginald Le Borg; Screenplay: Cyril Endfield, Albert DePina (Original Story: Hal E. Chester); Camera: Benjamin Kline; Music: Edward J. Kay; Editor: Bernard W. Burton; Art Director: Edward C. Jewell.

Cast: Leon Errol (Knobby Walsh); Elyse Knox (Anne); Joe Kirkwood, Jr. (Joe Palooka); Eduardo Cianelli (Florini); Joe Sawyer (Lefty); Elisha Cook, Jr. (Eugene); Sam McDaniel (Smoky); Robert Kent (Brewster); Sarah Padden (Mom Palooka); Michael Mark (Pop Palooka); Lou Nova (Al Costa); Russ Vincent (Curly); Alexander Laszlo (Aladar); Carole Dunne (Mrs. Oberlander); Carol Hughes (Mrs. Van Praag); Betty Blythe (Mrs. Stafford); Philip Van Zandt (Freddie Wells); Jimmy McLarnin (Referee); Joe Lewis, Manuel Ortiz, Caferino Garcia, Henry Armstrong, Jack Roper (Themselves).

JOE PALOOKA IN FIGHTING MAD (Monogram, 1948)—theatrical feature; 75 minutes.

Credits: Producer: Hal E. Chester; Director: Reginald Le Borg; Screenplay: John Bright (Original Story: Ralph S. Lewis, Bernard D. Shamberg; Additional Dialogue: Monte F. Collins).

Cast: Leon Errol; Joe Kirkwood; Elyse Knox; John Hubbard; Patricia Dane; Charles Lane; Wally Vernon; Frank Hyers; Jack Shea; Jack Roper; Horace McMahon; Jack Overman; Eddie Gribbon; Sarah Padden; Michael Mark; Evelynne Smith; Geneva Gray; Johnny Indrisano; Frank Reicher; Jay Norris; Paul Scardon; Virginia Belmont; Larry Steers; Robert Conway; Herb Vigran; Dewey Robinson; Emil Sitka; Murray Leonard; Robert C. McCracken; Cy Kendall; Bill McLean; Jack Mower; Paul Bryar; Sammy Wolfe; Reid Kilpatrick; Ted Pavelec.

JOE PALOOKA IN WINNER TAKE ALL (Monogram, 1948)—theatrical feature; 64 minutes.

Credits: Producer: Hal E. Chester; Director: Reginald Le Borg; Screenplay: Stanley Rubin, Monte V. Collins; Camera: William Sickner; Music: Edward J. Kay; Editor: Cecil Lovering; Art Director: Dave Milton.

Cast: Joe Kirkwood, Jr. (Joe Palooka); Elyse Knox (Anne Howe); William Frawley (Knobby Walsh); Stanley Clements (Tommy); John Shelton (Greg Tanner); Mary Beth Hughes (Millie); Sheldon Leonard (Herman); Frank Jenks (Looie); Lyle Talbot (Henderson); Jack Roper (Waldo); Eddie Gribbon (Canvas); Wally Vernon (Taxi Driver); Ralph Sanford (Lt. Steve Mulford); Bill Martin (Sportscaster); "Big" Ben Moroz (Bobo Walker); Hal Fieberling (Sammy Talbot); William Ruhl (Talbot's Manager); Chester Clute (Doniger); Douglas Fowley, Stanley Prager (Reporters); Hugh Charles, Forrest Matthews (Instructors); Gertrude Astor (Mrs. Howard); Hal Gerard (TV Announcer).

JOE PALOOKA IN THE BIG FIGHT (Monogram, 1949)— theatrical feature; 66 minutes.

Credits: Producer: Hal E. Chester; Director: Cyril Endfield; Screenplay: Stanley Prager, Cyril Endfield; Camera: Mark Stengler; Music: Edward Kay; Editor: Fred Maguire; Art Director: Dave Milton; Set Design: Raymond Boltz, Jr.; Fight Scenes Staged By: John Indrisano.

Cast: Leon Errol (Knobby Walsh); Joe Kirkwood, Jr. (Joe Palooka); Lina Romay (Maxine); David Bruce (Tom Conway); George O'Hanlon (Looie); Virginia Welles (Anne Howe); Greg McClure (Grady); Taylor Holmes (Dr. Benson); Ian McDonald (Mike); Lou Lubin (Talmadge); Bert Conway (Pee Wee); Lyle Talbot (Lieutenant Muldoon); Benny Baker (Flight Secretary); Eddie Gribbon (Canvas); Jack Roper (Scranton); Frances Osborne (Wardrobe Woman); Harry Hayden (Commissioner Harris); Frank Fenton (Detective); George Fisher (Contest Announcer); John Indrisano; Ted Pavelec.

JOE PALOOKA IN THE COUNTERPUNCH (Monogram, 1949)—theatrical feature; 74 minutes.

Credits: Producer: Hal E. Chester; Director: Reginald Le Borg; Screenplay: Henry Blankfort, Cyril Endfield; Camera: William Sickner; Music: Edward J. Kay; Editor: Warren Adams; Art Director: David Milton; Set Design: Raymond Boltz, Jr.

Cast: Leon Errol (Knobby Walsh); Joe Kirkwood, Jr. (Joe Palooka); Elyse Knox (Anne Howe); Marcel Journet (Anton Kindel); Sheila Ryan (Myra); Harry Lewis (Chick Bennett); Frank Sully (Looie); Ian Wolfe (Professor Lilliquist); Sam Hayes (Fight Announcer); Walter Sande (Austin); Douglas Dumbrille (Captain Lance); Douglas Fowley (Thurston); Eddie Gribbon (Canvasback); Suni Chorre (Cardona); Ralph Graves (Dr. Colman); Martin Garralaga (Announcer); Roland Dupree (Bell Boy); Gertrude Messinger (Nurse); John Hart (Pedro); Robert Conway (Steward); John Indrisano, Joe Herrera (Referees).

JOE PALOOKA IN HUMPHREY TAKES A CHANCE
(Monogram, 1950)—theatrical feature; 63 minutes.

Credits: Producer: Hal E. Chester; Director: Jean Yarbrough; Screenplay: Henry Blankfort.

Cast: Leon Errol; Joe Kirkwood; Pamela Blake; Robert Coogan; Jerome Cowan; Joe Besser; Don McGuire; Donald MacBride; Curt Bois; Clem Bevans; Frank Sully; Eddie Gribbon; Meyer Grace; Lillian Bronson; Sam Balter.

JOE PALOOKA IN THE SQUARED CIRCLE (Monogram, 1950)—theatrical feature; 63 minutes.

Credits: Producer: Hal E. Chester; Director: Reginald Le Borg; Screenplay: Jan Jeffrey (Original Story: B. F. Meltzer); Camera: Marcel Le Picard.

Cast: Joe Kirkwood, Jr. (Joe Palooka); James Gleason (Knobby Walsh); Lois Hall (Anne Howe); Edgar Barrier (Brogden); Myrna Dell (Sandra); Robert Coogan (Humphrey Pennyworth); Dan Seymour (Crawford); Charles Halton (Merkle); Frank Jenks (Looie); Greg McClure (Pete); Eddie Gribbon (Canvas); Robert Griffin (Kebo); John Harmon (Phillips); Jack Roper (Gunsel); Sue Carlton (Felice); William Haade (Bubbles); Stanley Prager (TV Announcer); Mervin Williams (Second Reporter); Hal Feiberling (Pinky Thompson); John Merrick (Tiny); Paul Bryar (Roderick).

JOE PALOOKA MEETS HUMPHREY (Monogram, 1950—theatrical feature; 65 minutes.

Credits: Producer: Hal E. Chester; Director: Jean Yarbrough; Screenplay: Henry Blankfort; Camera: William Sickner; Music: Edward J. Kay; Editor: Otho Lovering; Art Director: Dave Milton.

Cast: Leon Errol (Knobby Walsh/Lord Cecil Poole); Joe Kirkwood, Jr. (Joe Palooka); Robert Coogan (Humphrey); Jerome Cowan (Belden); Joe Besser (Carlton); Don McGuire (Mitchell); Pamela Blake (Anne Howe); Donald McBride (Mayor); Curt Bois (Pierre); Clem Bevans (Mr. Edwards); Frank Sully (Looie); Eddie Gribbon (Canvas); Meyer Grace (Referee); Lillian Bronson (Prunella); Sam Balter (Announcer); Frosty Royce; Russ Kaplan; Sandra Gould; Bert Conway; Ray Walker; Knox Manning.

JOE PALOOKA IN TRIPLE CROSS (Monogram, 1951)—theatrical feature; 60 minutes.

Credits: Producer: Hal E. Chester; Director: Reginald Le Borg; Screenplay: Jan Jeffrey (Original Story: Harold Bancroft); Camera: William Sickner; Music: Darrell Calker; Art Director: Martin Obzina.

Cast: Joe Kirkwood, Jr. (Joe Palooka); James Gleason (Knobby Walsh); Cathy Downs (Anne Howe); John Emery (The Professor); Steve Brodie (Dutch); Don Harvey (Chuck); Rufe Davis (Kenny Smith); Jimmy Wallington (Himself); Mary Young (Mrs. Reed); Eddie Gribbon (Canvas); Sid Tomack (Looie); Dickie Leroy (Bub); Jimmie Lloyd (Bill); Cliff Clark (Sheriff Malin); Hank Worden (Farmer).

THE JOE PALOOKA STORY (Syndicated, 1954)—TV series; each episode 30 minutes.

Cast: Joe Kirkwood, Jr. (Joe Palooka); Cathy Downs (Anne Howe); Luis Van Rooten, Sid Tomack (Knobby Walsh); "Slapsie" Maxie Rosenbloom (Humphrey Pennyworth).

Distributed by the McNaught Syndicate, this humor strip was created by Ham Fisher and first appeared in 1928.

The 1934 feature film starring Stuart Erwin remains the most interesting film adaptation, boasting an interesting cast that somewhat compensates for the dull pacing, with Jimmy Durante and Lupe Velez contributing memorable bits.

JON SABLE
comic book
First Comics

SABLE (ABC, 1987)—TV series; each episode 60 minutes; color.

Credits: Executive Producers: Richard P. Rosetti, Gary Sherman; Producers: Gary Sherman, Edward Ledding; Director: Gary Sherman; Screenplay: Gary Sherman; Camera: Alex Nepomniaschy; Music: Michael Shreive.

Cast: Lewis Van Bergen; Renée Russo; Ken Page; Holly Fulger; Marge Kotlisky; John Harkias; Tony Lincoln.

This cynical superhero character first appeared in JON SABLE #1 in June of 1983.

JUNGLE JIM
newspaper strip

JUNGLE JIM (Universal, 1937)—theatrical serial; 12 chapters, approximately 20 minutes each.

Credits: Directors: Forde Beebe, Cliff Smith; Screenplay: Wyndham Gittens, Norman S. Hall, Ray Trampe; Camera: Jerry Ash.

Cast: Grant Withers (Jungle Jim); Betty Jane Rhodes (Joan); Raymond Hatton (Malay Mike); Henry Brandon (The Cobra); Evelyn Brent (Shanghai Lil); Bryant Washburn (Bruce Redmond); Selmer Jackson (Tyler); Al Bridge (Slade); Paul Sutton (La Bat); Al Duvall (Kolu); William Royale (Hawks).

Chapter Titles: (1) Into the Lion's Den; (2) The Cobra Strikes; (3) The Menacing Herd; (4) The Killer's Trail; (5) The Bridge of Terror; (6) Drums of Doom; (7) The Earth Trembles; (8) The Killer Lion; (9) The Devil Bird; (10) Descending Doom; (11) In the Cobra's Castle; (12) The Last Safari.

JUNGLE JIM (Columbia, 1948)—theatrical feature; 71 minutes.

Credits: Producer: Sam Katzman; Director: William Berke; Screenplay: Carroll Young; Camera: Lester White; Editor:

Aaron Stell; Music: Mischa Bakaleinikoff; Art Director: Paul Palmentola.

Cast: Johnny Weissmuller (Jungle Jim); Virginia Grey (Hilary Parker); George Reeves (Bruce Edwards); Lita Baron (Zia); Rick Vallin (Kolu); Holmes Herbert (Commissioner Marsden); Tex Mooney (Chief Devil Doctor).

THE LOST TRIBE (Columbia, 1949)—theatrical feature; 72 minutes.

Credits: Producer: Sam Katzman; Director: William Berke; Screenplay: Arthur Hoerl, Don Martin (Original Story: Arthur Hoerl); Camera: Ira H. Morgan; Editor: Aaron Stell; Music: Mischa Bakaleinikoff; Art Director: Paul Palmentola.

Cast: Johnny Weissmuller (Jungle Jim); Myrna Dell (Norina); Elena Verdugo (Li Wanna); Joseph Vitale (Calhoun); Ralph Dunn (Captain Rawling); Paul Marion (Chot); Nelson Leigh (Zoron); Geroge J. Lewis (Whip Wilson); Gil Perkins (Dojek); George DeNormand (Cullen); Wally West (Eckle); Rube Schaffer (Lerch).

CAPTIVE GIRL (Columbia, 1950)—theatrical feature; 73 minutes.

Credits: Producer: Sam Katzman; Director: William Berke; Screenplay: Carroll Young; Camera: Ira H. Morgan; Music: Mischa Bakaleinikoff; Editor: Henry Batista; Art Director: Paul Palmentola.

Cast: Johnny Weissmuller (Jungle Jim); Buster Crabbe (Barton); Anita Lhoest (Joan); Rick Vallin (Mahala); John Dehner (Hakim); Rusty Wescoatt (Silva); Nelson Leigh (Missionary).

DEVIL GODDESS (Columbia, 1950)—theatrical feature; 70 minutes.

Credits: Producer: Sam Katzman; Director: Spencer G. Bennet; Screenplay: George Plympton (Original Story: Dwight Babcock); Camera: Ira H. Morgan; Music: Mischa Bakaleinikoff; Art Director: Paul Palmentola; Editor: Aaron Stell.

Cast: Johnny Weissmuller (Himself); Angela Stevens (Nora Blakely); Selmer Jackson (Professor Carl Blakely); William Tannen (Nels Comstock); Ed Hinton (Joseph Leopold); William M. Griffith (Ralph Dixon); Frank Lackteen (Nikruma); Abel M. Fernandez (Teinusi); Vera M. Francis (Serab'na); George Berkely (Bert).

MARK OF THE GORILLA (Columbia, 1950)—theatrical feature; 68 minutes.

Credits: Producer: Sam Katzman; Director: William Berke; Screenplay: Carroll Young; Camera: Ira H. Morgan; Editor: Henry Batista; Music: Mischa Bakaleinikoff; Art Direction: Paul Palmentola.

Cast: Johnny Weissmuller (Jungle Jim); Trudy Marshall (Barbara Bentley); Suzanne Dalbert (Nyobi); Onslow Stevens (Brandt); Robert Purcell (Kramer); Pierce Lyden (Gibbs); Neyle Morrow (Head Ranger); Selmer Jackson (Warden Bentley).

PYGMY ISLAND (Columbia, 1950)—theatrical feature; 69 minutes.

Credits: Producer: Sam Katzman; Director: William Berke; Screenplay: Carroll Young; Camera: Ira H. Morgan; Editor:

PYGMY ISLAND (Columbia, 1950): Johnny Weissmuller cavorts with a sarong-clad Columbia starlet.

Jerome Thomas; Music: Mischa Bakaleinikoff; Art Director: Paul Palmentola.

Cast: Johnny Weissmuller (Jungle Jim); Ann Savage (Captain Ann Kingsley); David Bruce (Major Bolton); Steven Geray (Leon Marko); William Tannan (Kruger); Tristram Coffin (Novak); Billy Curtis (Makuba); Tommy Farrell (Captain); Pierce Lyden (Lucas); Rusty Wescoatt (Anders); Billy Barty (Tembo).

FURY OF THE CONGO (Columbia, 1951)—theatrical feature; 69 minutes.

Credits: Producer: Sam Katzman; Director: William Berke; Screenplay: Carroll Young; Camera: Ira H. Morgan; Editor:

Richard Fantl; Music: Mischa Bakaleinikoff; Art Direction: Paul Palmentola.

Cast: Johnny Weissmuller (Jungle Jim); Sherry Moreland (Leta); William Henry (Ronald Cameron); Lyle Talbot (Grant); Joel Friedkin (Professor Dunham); George Eldredge (Barnes); Rusty Wescoatt (Magruder); Paul Marion (Raadi); Bianca Vischer (Mahara); Pierce Lyden (Allen); John Hart (Guard).

JUNGLE MANHUNT (Columbia, 1951)—theatrical feature; 66 minutes.

Credits: Producer: Sam Katzman; Director: Lew Landers; Screenplay: Samuel Newman; Camera: William Whitley; Editor: Henry Batista; Music: Mischa Bakaleinikoff; Art Director: Paul Palmentola.

Cast: Johnny Weissmuller (Jungle Jim); Bob Waterfield (Bob Miller); Sheila Ryan (Ann Lawrence); Rick Vallin (Bono); Lyle Talbot (Dr. Mitchell Heller); William P. Wilkerson (Maklee Chief); Tamba (Himself).

JUNGLE JIM IN THE FORBIDDEN LAND (Columbia, 1952)—theatrical feature; 64 minutes.

Credits: Producer: Sam Katzman; Director: Lew Landers; Screenplay: Samual Newman; Camera: Fayte M. Brown, Editor: Henry Batista; Music: Mischa Bakaleinikoff; Art Director: Paul Palmentola.

Cast: Johnny Weissmuller (Jungle Jim); Angela Greene (Linda Roberts); Jean Wiles (Denise); Lester Matthews (Commissioner Kingston); William Tannen (Doc Edwards); George Eldredge (Fred Lewis); Frederic Berest (Zulu); Clem Erickson

(Giant Man); Irmgard H. H. Raschke (Giant Woman); William Fawcett (Old One); Frank Jacquet (Quigley); Tamba (Himself).

VOODOO TIGER (Columbia, 1952)—theatrical feature; 67 minutes.

Credits: Producer: Sam Katzman; Director: Spencer Bennet; Screenplay: Samuel Newman; Camera: William Whitley; Editor: Gene Havlick; Music: Mischa Bakaleinikoff; Art Director: Paul Palmentola; Set Decorator: Sidney Clifford.

Cast: Johnny Weissmuller (Jungle Jim); Jean Byron (Phyllis Bruce); James Seay (Abel Peterson); Jeanne Dean (Shalimar); Charles Horvath (Wombulu); Robert Bray (Major Bill Green); Michael Fox (Carl Werner); John Cason (Jerry Masters); Paul Hoffman (Michael Kovacs); Richard Kipling (Commissioner Kingston); Frederic Berest (Native Chief); William B. Klein (Co-Pilot); Alex Montoya (Native Leader); Rick Vallin (Sergeant Bono); Tamba (Himself).

KILLER APE (Columbia, 1953)—theatrical feature; 68 minutes.

Credits: Producer: Sam Katzman; Director: Spencer Gordon Bennet; Screenplay: Carroll Young, Arthur Hoerl (Original Story: Carroll Young); Camera: William Whitley; Editor: Gene Havlick; Music: Mischa Bakaleinikoff; Art Director: Paul Palmentola.

Cast: Johnny Weissmuller (Jungle Jim); Carol Thurston (Shari); Max Palmer (Man-Ape); Burt Wenland (Ramada); Nestor Paiva (Andrews); Paul Marton (Mahara); Eddie Foster (Achmed); Rory Mallinson (Perry); Ray Corrigan (Norley); Nick Stuart (Maron); Tamba (Himself).

SAVAGE MUTINY (Columbia, 1953)—theatrical feature; 73 minutes.

Credits: Producer: Sam Katzman; Director: Spencer Gordon Bennet; Screenplay: Sol Shor; Camera: William Whitley; Editor: Henry Batista; Music: Mischa Bakaleinikoff; Art Director: Paul Palmentola.

Cast: Johnny Weissmuller (Jungle Jim); Angela Stevens (Joan Harris); Lester Matthews (Major Walsh); Nelson Leigh (Dr. Parker); Charles Stevens (Chief Wamai); Paul Marion (Lutembi); Gregory Gay (Carl Kroman); Leonard Penn (Emil Bruno); Ted Thorpe (Paul Benek); George Robotham (Johnson); Tamba (Himself).

VALLEY OF THE HEADHUNTERS (Columbia, 1953)—theatrical feature; 67 minutes.

Credits: Producer: Sam Katzman; Director: William Berke; Screenplay: Samuel Newman; Camera: William Whitley; Editor: Gene Havlick; Music: Mischa Bakaleinikoff; Art Director: Paul Palmentola.

Cast: Johnny Weissmuller (Jungle Jim); Christine Lawson (Ellen Shaw); Robert C. Foulk (Arco); Steven Ritch (Lieutenant Barry); Nelson Leigh (Mr. Bradley); Joseph Allen, Jr. (Pico Church); George Eldredge (Commissioner Kingston); Neyle Morrow (Corporal Bono); Vince M. Townsend, Jr. (M'Gono); Don Blackman (Chief Bagava); Paul Thompson (Chief Gitzhak); Tamba (Himself).

CANNIBAL ATTACK (Columbia, 1954)—theatrical feature; 69 minutes.

Credits: Producer: Sam Katzman; Director: Lee Sholem; Screenplay: Carroll Young; Camera: Henry Freulich; Music: Mischa Bakaleinikoff; Editor: Edwin Bryant.

Cast: Johnny Weissmuller (Himself); Judy Walsh (Luora); David Bruce (Arnold King); Bruce Cowling (Rovak); Charles Evans (Commissioner); Steve Darrell (John King); Joseph A. Allen, Jr. (Jason).

JUNGLE MAN-EATERS (Columbia, 1954)—theatrical feature; 67 minutes.

Credits: Producer: Sam Katzman; Director: Lee Sholem; Screenplay: Samuel Newman; Camera: Henry Freulich; Editor: George Havlick; Music: Mischa Bakaleinikoff; Art Director: Paul Palmentola.

Cast: Johnny Weissmuller (Jungle Jim); Karin Booth (Bonnie); Richard Stapley (Bernard); Bernard Hamilton (Zuwaba); Lester Matthews (Commissioner Kingston); Paul Thompson (Zulu); Vince M. Townsend, Jr. (Chief Boganda); Louise Franklin (N'Gala); Gregory Gay (Latour); Tamba (Himself).

JUNGLE MOON MEN (Columbia, 1955)—theatrical feature; 69 minutes.

Credits: Producer: Sam Katzman; Director: Charles S. Gould; Screenplay: Dwight V. Babcock, Jo Pagano (Original Story: Jo Pagano); Camera: Henry Freulich; Editor: Henry Batista; Music: Mischa Bakaleinikoff; Art Director: Paul Palmentola.

Cast: Johnny Weissmuller (Himself); Jean Byron (Ellen Marston); Helen Stanton (Oma); Bill Henry (Bob Prentice); Myron Healey (Mark Santo); Billy Curtis (Damu); Michael

Granger (Nolima); Frank Sully (Max); Benjamin F. Chapman, Jr. (Marro); Kenneth L. Smith (Link); Ed Hinton (Regan).

JUNGLE JIM (Syndicated, 1955)—TV series; 26 episodes, 30 minutes each.

Credits: Producer: Harold Greene; Director: Don McDougall; Music: Alec Compinsky.

Cast: Johnny Weissmuller (Jungle Jim); Martin Huston (Skipper); Norman Fredric (Kaseem); Peggy (Tamba).

Distributed by King Features Syndicate, this jungle-adventure strip was created by Alex Raymond as a back-up companion strip (appearing at the bottom of the same page) with FLASH GORDON, and premiered with the space-adventure strip in January of 1934.

The 1937 Universal Pictures serial adaptation has remained unseen since its original release. The Columbia features, produced by Sam Katzman and starring Johnny Weissmuller, were, at best, efficiently produced "B" movie fodder, with Weissmuller never straying far from a rear-projection screen as he goes through his wooden paces in front of every foot of grainy stock jungle footage Katzman was able to excavate from the Columbia Pictures vaults.

KING OF THE ROYAL MOUNTED
newspaper strip

KING OF THE ROYAL MOUNTED (Republic, 1940)—theatrical serial; 12 chapters, first chapter approximately 30 minutes, remaining chapters approximately 20 minutes each.

Credits: Associate Producer: Hiram S. Brown, Jr.; Directors: William Witney, John English; Screenplay: Franklyn Adreon, Norman S. Hall, Joseph Poland, Barney A. Sarecky, Sol Shor; Camera: William Nobles; Music: Cy Feuer; Editors: Edward Todd, William Thompson.

Cast: Allan Lane (Sergeant King); Robert Strange (Kettler); Robert Kellard (Cpl. Tom Merritt, Jr.); Lita Conway (Linda Merrit); Herbert Rawlinson (Inspector King); Harry Cording (Wade Garson); Bryant Washburn (Crandall); Budd Buster (Vinegar Smith); Stanley Andrews (Merritt, Sr.); John Davidson (Dr. Shelton); John Dilson (Dr. Wall); Paul McVey (Excellency Zarnoff); Lucien Prival (Admiral Johnson); Norman Willis (Captain Tarner); Tony Paton (Le Couteau).

Chapter Titles: (1) Man Hunt; (2) Winged Death; (3) Boomerang; (4) Devil Doctor; (5) Sabotage; (6) False Ransom; (7) Death Tunes In; (8) Satan's Cauldron; (9) Espionage; (10) Blazing Guns; (11) Master Spy; (12) Code of the Mounted.

Notes: A seven-reel feature version entitled THE YUKON PATROL was released by Republic in 1942.

KING OF THE MOUNTIES (Republic, 1942)—theatrical serial; 12 chapters, first chapter approximately 30 minutes, remaining chapters approximately 20 minutes each.

Credits: Associate Producer: William J. O'Sullivan; Director: William Witney; Screenplay: Ronald Davidson, William Lively, Joseph O'Donnell, Joseph Poland; Camera: Bud Thackery; Music: Mort Glickman; Special Effects: Howard Lydecker.

Cast: Allan Lane (Dave King); Gilbert Emery (Morrison); Russell Hicks (Carleton); Peggy Drake (Carol Brent); George Irving (Marshall Brent); Abner Biberman (Yamata); William

Vaughn (Von Horst); Nestor Paiva (Baroni); Bradley Page (Charles Blake); Douglass Dumbrille (Gil Harper); William Bakewell (Hal Ross); Duncan Renaldo (Pierre); Francis Ford (Zeke Collins); Jay Novello (Lewis); Anthony Warde (Starke); Norman Nesbitt (Newscaster); John Hiestand (Lane); Allen Jung (Sato); Paul Fung (Bombardier); Arvon Dale (Craig).

Chapter Titles: (1) Phantom Invaders; (2) Road to Death; (3) Human Target; (4) Railroad Saboteurs; (5) Suicide Dive; (6) Blazing Barrier; (7) Perilous Plunge; (8) Electrocuted; (9) Reign of Terror; (10) The Flying Coffin; (11) Deliberate Murder; (12) On to Victory.

Distributed by King Features Syndicate, this Mountie-adventure strip was created by famed western author Zane Grey and artist Allen Dean. The first installment appeared in February of 1935 and the strip ran until it was discontinued in March of 1955.

LET GEORGE DO IT
newspaper strip

LET GEORGE DO IT theatrical short subjects.

The following two-reelers were all released by Universal Pictures. These titles have been confirmed. There may be other entries in the series that are unknown.

AND GEORGE DID! (1926); BACKWARD GEORGE (1926); BY GEORGE (1926); GEORGE IN LOVE (1926); GEORGE RUNS WILD (1926); GEORGE THE WINNER (1926); WHY GEORGE! (1926); BIG GAME GEORGE (1927); DISOR-DERED ORDERLY (1927); GEORGE LEAVES HOME

(1927); GEORGE MEETS GEORGE (1927); GEORGE STEPS OUT (1927); GEORGE'S MANY LOVES (1927); GEORGE'S SCHOOL DAZE (1927); HIGH FLYIN' GEORGE (1927); KID GEORGE (1927); MAN OF LETTERS (1927); MODEL GEORGE (1927); OH, TAXI! (1927); ON DECK (1927); ON FURLOUGH (1927); PICKING ON GEORGE (1927); RUSHING BUSINESS (1927); WATCH, GEORGE! (1927); WHEN GEORGE HOPS (1927); ALL FOR GERALDINE (1928); CRUSHED HATS (1928); GEORGE'S FALSE ALARM (1928); HOT PUPPIES (1928); LOOK PLEASANT (1928); RUBBER NECKS (1928); SAILOR GEORGE (1928); CLOSE SHAVES (1929); CUT-UPS (1929); FLY COPS (1929); PRIVATE BUSINESS (1929); TELEVISION GEORGE (1929).

This humor strip was created by George McManus for Pulitzer's *New York World* in 1904. A series of two-reelers was produced by the Stern brothers for Universal Pictures.

LI'L ABNER
newspaper strip

LI'L ABNER (RKO, 1940)—theatrical feature; 78 minutes (*GB:* TROUBLE CHASERS).

Credits: Producer: Herman Schlom; Director: Albert S. Rogell; Screenplay: Charles Kerr, Tyler Johnson; Music and Lyrics: Ben Oakland, Milton Drake, Milton Berle.

Cast: Granville Owne (Li'l Abner); Martha O'Driscoll (Daisy Mae); Mona Ray (Mammy Yokum); Johnnie Morris (Pappy Yokum); Buster Keaton (Lonesome Polecat); Billie Seward (Cousin Delightful); Kay Sutton (Wendy Wilecat); Maude Eburne (Granny Scraggs); Edgar Kennedy (Cornelius Cornpone); Charles A. Post (Earthquake McGoon); Bud Jamison (Hairless Joe); Dick Elliott (Marryin' Sam); Johnny Arthur; Walter Catlett; Lucien Littlefield; Frank Wilder; Chester Conklin; Mickey Daniels; Doodles Weaver.

LI'L ABNER (NBC, 1949)—unsold TV pilot; running time unknown.

Cast: Gregg Palmer (Li'l Abner); Marilyn Monroe (Daisy Mae).

Notes: Al Capp and Busby Berkeley were also involved with this unsold pilot.

LI'L ABNER (Paramount, 1959)—theatrical feature; 113 minutes; color.

Credits: Producer: Norman Panama; Director: Melvin Frank; Screenplay: Norman Panama, Melvin Frank; Camera: Daniel L. Fapp; Editor: Arthur P. Schmidt; Art Directors: Hal Pereira, J. MacMillan Johnson; Special Effects: John P. Fulton; Music: Nelson Riddle; Music Direction: Joseph Lilley, Nelson Riddle; Songs ("Jubilation T. Cornpone," "Don't Take That Rag Off'n the Bush," "A Typical Day," "If I Had My Druthers," "Room Enuff for Us," "Namely You," "The Country's in the Very Best of Hands," "Unnecessary Town," "I'm Past My Prime," "I Wish It Could Be Otherwise," "Put 'em Back the Way They Wuz," "Matrimonial Stomp"): Gene De Paul, Johnny Mercer; Choreography: Michael Kidd, Dee Dee Wood.

Cast: Peter Palmer (Li'l Abner); Leslie Parrish (Daisy Mae); Stubby Kaye (Marryin' Sam); Julie Newmar (Stupefyin' Jones); Howard St. John (General Bullmoose); Stella Stevens (Appassionata Von Climax); Billie Hayes (Mammy Yokum); Joe E. Marks (Pappy Yokum); Bern Hoffman (Earthquake

LI'L ABNER (Paramount, 1959): Peter Palmer, Stubby Kaye, Leslie Parrish.

McGoon); Al Nesor (Evil Eye Fleagle); Robert Strauss (Romeo Scragg); William Lanteau (Available Jones); Ted Thurston (Sen. Jack S. Phogbound); Carmen Alvarez (Moonbeam McSwine); Alan Carney (Mayor Dawgmeat); Stanley Simmonds (Rasmussen T. Finsdale); Joe Ploski; Diki Lerner.

LI'L ABNER (NBC, 1967)—TV pilot; 30 minutes; color.

Credits: Producer: Howard Leeds; Director: Coby Ruskin; Screenplay: Al Capp.

Cast: Sammy Jackson (Li'l Abner); Jeannine Riley (Daisy Mae); Judy Canova (Mammy Yokum); Jerry Lester (Pappy Yokum); Robert Reed (Senator Cod).

LI'L ABNER (NBC, 1971)—TV special; 60 minutes; color.

Credits: Producers: Allan Blye, Chris Bearde; Director: Gordon Wiles; Screenplay: Coslough Johnson, Ted Ziegler, Allan Blye, Chris Bearde.

Cast: Ray Young (Li'l Abner); Nancee Parkinson (Daisy Mae); Billie Hayes (Mammy Yokum); Billy Bletcher (Pappy Yokum); Dale Malone (Marryin' Sam); Bobo Lewis (Nightmare Alice); Ken Berry; Eddie Albert; Carol Burnett; Monty Hall; Donald O'Connor.

Initially distributed by United Features Syndicate and later picked up by the New York News Syndicate, writer/artist Al Capp's famous humor strip first appeared in August of 1934.

The trenchant satire of Capp's creation has consistently escaped Hollywood, with the two features adapted from the strip concentrating instead on the more obvious humorous aspects of Capp's hillbilly characters.

The RKO version of 1940 is by far the more acceptable of the two films but was unsuccessful, and some of the characters, outfitted with rubber facial appliances in an attempt to render Capp's visual designs faithfully, look more like refugees from a horror movie. The Paramount musical version of two decades later is lavish and over-produced, based on a hit Broadway musical version of the period. Seen today, the film seems like a portent of later big-budget clunkers like POPEYE, offering a huge budget and precious little else in terms of creativity and charm.

LITTLE IODINE
newspaper strip

LITTLE IODINE (United Artists, 1946)—theatrical feature; 57 minutes.

LITTLE IODINE (United Artists, 1946): Jo Ann Marlowe in the title role.

Credits: Producers: Buddy Rogers, Ralph Cohn; Director: Reginald Le Borg; Screenplay: Richard Landau; Camera: Robert Pittack; Music: Alexander Steinert; Editor: Lynn Harrison; Art Director: George Van Marter.

Cast: Jo Ann Marlowe (Little Iodine); Marc Cramer (Marc Andrews); Eve Whitney (Janis Payne); Irene Ryan (Mrs. Tremble); Lanny Rees (Horace); Leon Belasco (Simkins); Emory Parnell (Mr. Bigdome); Sarah Selby (Mrs. Bigdome); Jean Patriguin (Grandma Jones).

Created by Jimmy Hatlo for his strip THEY'LL DO IT EVERY TIME, distributed by King Features Syndicate, the Little Iodine character, a physically repulsive, mischief-prone little girl, was so mysteriously popular that she was awarded her own strip in 1943.

LITTLE ORPHAN ANNIE
newspaper strip

LITTLE ORPHAN ANNIE (RKO, 1932)—theatrical feature; 60 minutes.

Credits: Director: John Robertson; Screenplay: Wanda Tuchock, Tom McNamara; Camera: Jack McKenzie.

Cast: Mitzi Green (Annie); Buster Phelps (Mickey); May Robson (Mrs. Stewart); Kate Lawson (Mrs. Burgin); Matt Moore (Dr. Griffith); Edgar Kennedy (Daddy Warbucks); Sidney Bracey (Butler).

LITTLE ORPHAN ANNIE (Colonial/Paramount, 1938)—theatrical feature; 57 minutes.

LITTLE ORPHAN ANNIE (RKO, 1932): Mitzi Green, *right,* in the title role, evidently expressing her opinion of the script.

Credits: Producer: John Speaks; Director: Ben Holmes; Screenplay: Budd Schulberg, Samuel Ornitz (Original Story: Samuel Ornitz, Endre Bohem); Camera: Frank Redman; Editor: Robert Bischoff; Music: Lou Forbes; Art Director: Feild Gray.

Cast: Ann Gillis (Annie); Robert Kent (Johnny Adams); June Travis (Mary Ellen); J. Farrell MacDonald (Pop Corrigan); J. M. Kerrigan (Tom Jennings); Sarah Padden (Mrs. Moriarity); James Burke (Mike Moriarity); Ian MacLaren (Soo Long); Margaret Armstrong (Mrs. Jennings); Dorothy Vaughn (Mrs. Milligan); Ben Welden (Spot McGee).

ANNIE (Columbia, 1982)—theatrical feature; 130 minutes; color.

Credits: Producer: Ray Stark; Director: John Huston; Screenplay: Carol Sobieski (Original Stage Production Book: Thomas Meehan, Charles Strouse, Martin Charnin); Camera: Richard Moore; Editor: Michael A. Stevenson; Production Design: Dale Hennesy; Art Directors: Robert Guerra, Diane Wager; Costumes: Theoni V. Aldredge; Choreography: Arlene Phillips; Music and Lyrics (for the song "Tomorrow"): Charles Strouse, Martin Charnin.

Cast: Albert Finney (Daddy Warbucks); Carol Burnett (Mrs. Hannigan); Bernadette Peters (Lily); Ann Reinking (Grace Farrell); Tim Curry (Rooster); Aileen Quinn (Annie); Geoffrey Holder (Punjab); Roger Minami (Asp); Toni Ann Gisandi (Molly); Rosanne Sorrentino (Pepper); Lara Berk (Tessie); April Lerman (Kate); Lucie Stewart (Duffy); Robin Ignito (July); Edward Herrmann (FDR); Lois De Banzie (Eleanor Roosevelt); Peter Marshall (Bert Healy); Loni Ackerman, Murphy Cross, Nancy Sinclair (Boylan Sisters); I. M. Hobson (Drake); Lu Leonard (Mrs. Pugh); Marvis Ray (Mrs. Greer); Pam Blair (Annette); Colleen Zenk (Celeste); Victor Griffin

(Saunders); Jerome Collamore (Frick); Jon Richards (Frack); Wayne Cilento (Photographer); Ken Swofford (Weasel).

Distributed by the Chicago Tribune-New York News Syndicate, LITTLE ORPHAN ANNIE was created by Harold Gray, the first strip appearing in August of 1924.

There were two negligible feature-film adaptations in the 1930s, and in 1982 the hit Broadway musical version was adapted to film and directed (quite badly) by John Huston.

MANDRAKE, THE MAGICIAN
newspaper strip

MANDRAKE, THE MAGICIAN (Columbia, 1939)—theatrical serial; 12 chapters, first chapter approximately 30 minutes, remaining chapters approximately 20 minutes each.

Credits: Producer: Jack Fier; Directors: Sam Nelson, Norman Deming; Screenplay: Joseph F. Poland, Basil Dickey, Ned Dandy; Camera: Ben Kline; Music: Lee Zahler; Editor: Richard Fantl; Sound: Edward Bernds.

Cast: Warren Hull (Mandrake); Doris Weston (Betty); Al Kikume (Lothar); Rex Downing (Tommy); Edward Earle (André); Forbes Murray (Houston); Kenneth MacDonald (Webster); Don Beddoe (Raymond); Dick Curtis (Dorgan); John Tyrrell (Dirk); Ernie Adams (Brown); George Chesebro (Baker); George Turner (Hall).

Chapter Titles: (1) Shadow on the Wall; (2) Trap of The Wasp; (3) City of Terror; (4) The Secret Passage; (5) The Devil's Playmate; (6) The Final Crash; (7) Gamble for Life; (8) Across the Deadline; (9) Terror Rides the Rails; (10) The

MANDRAKE, THE MAGICIAN (Columbia, 1939): Warren Hull, *center*, receives a mysterious package. Hopefully, it will contain a better script.

Unseen Monster; (11) At the Stroke of Eight; (12) The Reward of Treachery.

MANDRAKE, THE MAGICIAN (1954)—syndicated TV series; each episode 30 minutes.

Cast: Coe Norton (Mandrake); Woody Strode (Lothar).

MANDRAKE (NBC, 1979)—TV movie; 120 minutes; color.

Credits: Producer: Rick Husky; Director: Harry Falk; Screenplay: Rick Husky; Camera: Vincent A. Martinelli; Art Director: John Bruce; Music: Morton Stevens.

Cast: Anthony Herrera (Mandrake); Ji-Tu Cumbuka (Lothar); Simone Griffeth (Stacy); Gretchen Corbett (Jennifer Lindsay); Peter Haskell (William Romero); David Hooks (Dr. Malcolm Lindsay); Harry Blackstone, Jr. (Dr. Nolan); Hank Branst (Alex Gordon).

Created by writer Lee Falk and artist Phil Davis for King Features Syndicate, this fantasy-adventure strip about a heroic magician premiered in June of 1934.

There is precious little fantasy or heroism to be found in the Columbia Pictures serial adaptation of the strip, and this cliffhanger stands as one of that studios weakest efforts in the field. Even Warren Hull, a talented and entertaining actor who was excellent as the hero in the serial THE SPIDER'S WEB (1938), which was also made for Columbia, is ineffective as Mandrake. As the title hero pursues the villainous criminal The Wasp through twelve largely inert chapters, the bland proceedings finally sputter to a halt with one of the lamest conclusions of any serial in the sound era. "You're insane!" righteously proclaims Mandrake, as he finally confronts The Wasp in his lair. "That's your point of view!" The Wasp succinctly retorts, leaving the hapless viewer to ponder the colossal waste of time the previous twelve episodes represent.

MICKEY McGUIRE (THE TOONERVILLE FOLKS)
newspaper strip

MICKEY McGUIRE (THE TOONERVILLE FOLKS)— theatrical short subjects.

The following shorts were released by Associated First-National:

BOOS-EM FRIENDS (1921); THE SKIPPER HAS HIS FLING (1921); THE SKIPPER'S SCHEME (1921); THE SKIPPER'S TREASURE GARDEN (1921); THE TOONERVILLE FOLLIES (1921); TOONERVILLE TACTICS (1921); TOONERVILLE TANGLE (1921); THE TOONERVILLE TROLLEY THAT MEETS ALL TRAINS (1921).

Released by R-C Pictures Corp.:

MICKEY'S BATTLE (1927); MICKEY'S CIRCUS (1927); MICKEY'S PALS (1927).

Released by F.B.O. Prods., Inc.:

MICKEY'S ELEVEN (1927); MICKEY IN SCHOOL (1928); MICKEY'S LITTLE EVA (1928); MICKEY'S PARADE (1928).

Released by Standard Cinema Corp.:

MICKEY THE DETECTIVE (1928); MICKEY'S ATHLETES (1928); MICKEY'S BIG GAME HUNT (1928); MICKEY'S MOVIES (1928); MICKEY'S RIVALS (1928); MICKEY'S BROWN DERBY (1929); MICKEY'S EXPLORERS (1929); MICKEY'S GREAT IDEA (1929); MICKEY'S INITIATION (1929); MICKEY'S LAST CHANCE (1929); MICKEY'S MENAGERIE (1929); MICKEY'S MIDNITE FOLLIES (1929); MICKEY'S MIXUP (1929); MICKEY'S NORTHWEST MOUNTED (1929); MICKEY'S SURPRISE (1929); MICKEY'S MERRY MEN (1930); MICKEY'S MUSKETEERS (1930); MICKEY'S STRATEGY (1930); MICKEY'S WINNERS (1930); MICKEY'S CRUSADERS (1931); MICKEY'S DIPLOMACY (1931); MICKEY'S HELPING HAND (1931); MICKEY'S REBELLION (1931); MICKEY'S SIDELINE (1931); MICKEY'S STAMPEDE (1931); MICKEY'S HOLIDAY (1932).

Note: Mickey Rooney played Mickey McGuire in the MICKEY McGUIRE shorts.

Created by Fontaine Fox for the Wheeler Syndicate in 1915 and running until 1955, this popular strip, with its country setting, was a gentle satire of rural America. THE TOONERVILLE FOLKS was so widely read that the famous Toonerville Trolley was merchandised as a toy, and the eccentric characters in the strip were so incisively rendered that their fictional names became nationally famous. A series of silent shorts spawned the later MICKEY McGUIRE series starring Mickey Rooney, which ran well into the sound era.

MODESTY BLAISE
newspaper strip

MODESTY BLAISE (Twentieth Century-Fox, 1966)— theatrical feature; 118 minutes; color.

Credits: Producer: Joseph Janni; Director: Joseph Losey; Screenplay: Evan Jones (Original Story: Peter O'Donnell, Stanley Dubens); Camera: Jack Hildyard; Music: John Dankworth; Editor: Reginald Beck; Production Design: Richard MacDonald; Art Director: Jack Shampan; Costumes: Beatrice Dawson, Douglas Hayward, Marissa Martelli; Makeup: Neville Smallwood, Marissa Martelli.

Cast: Monica Vitti (Modesty Blaise); Terence Stamp (Willie Garvin); Dirk Bogarde (Gabriel); Harry Andrews (Sir Gerald Tarrant); Michael Craig (Paul Hagan); Clive Revill (McWhirter/ Sheik Abu Tahir); Alexander Knox (Minister); Rosella Falk (Mrs. Fothergill); Scilla Gabel (Melina); Michael Chow (Weng); Joe Melia (Crevier); Saro Urzi (Basilio); Tina Marquand (Nicole); Oliver MacGreevy (Tattooed Man); Jon Bluming

(Hans); Lex Schoorel (Walter); Marcello Turilli (Strauss); Giuseppe Paganelli (Friar); Wolfgang Hillinger (Handsome); Roberto Bisacco (Enrico); John Karlsen (Oleg); Silvan (The Great Pacco); John Stacy (Tyboria Captain); Robin Hunter (Pilot); Denys Graham (Co-Pilot); Patrick Ludlow (Under Secretary); Robin Fox (Man Who Pushes the Doorbell); George Fisher.

Created in 1963 by writer Peter O'Donnell and artist Jim Holdaway for the Beaverbrook Newspapers, this spy adventure strip dealt with the escapades of a beautiful female James Bond–type character.

MUTT & JEFF
newspaper strip

Created by Bud Fisher, this humor strip (originally titled A. MUTT) first appeared in November of 1907. Initially distributed by the Hearst Syndicate, the strip was later distributed by, variously, the Wheeler Syndicate, the Bell Syndicate, the Bell-McClure Syndicate, and the United Features Syndicate. Producers William and David Horsley, purveyors of film comedy, formed Nestor Films in 1910 and signed exclusive contracts with cartoonists Bud Fisher and Harry Hershfield, who created the DESPERATE DESMOND strip. Fisher served as an advisor on the resulting MUTT & JEFF films, with other hands involved in the actual scripting. Oddly, these short little silent films were billed as "talking pictures," with the dialogue *superimposed* over the picture at the bottom of the screen, instead of being inserted normally on title cards. The actors' names were never revealed to the public. Beginning with MUTT AND JEFF ON THE JOB in July of 1911, thirteen one-reel and twelve "split-reel" (running less than ten minutes) MUTT & JEFF shorts were made until November of 1911, when the DESPERATE DESMOND series, adapted from the Harry Hershfield cartoons, began. Six split-reel live-action shorts were derived from Hershfield's comical strip about a Victorian-age villain, but both series were discontinued (after netting profits of $60,000) in favor of more substantial dramatic fare.

THE NEWLYWEDS (BABY SNOOKUMS)
newspaper strip

THE NEWLYWEDS (BABY SNOOKUMS)—theatrical short subjects.

The following shorts were all released by Universal Pictures. These titles have been confirmed. There may be other entries in the series that are unknown.

FISHING SNOOKUMS (1926); THE NEWLYWEDS BUILD (1926); NEWLYWEDS' NEIGHBORS (1926); NEWLYWEDS QUARANTINED (1926); SNOOKUMS' BUGGY RIDE (1926); SNOOKUMS CLEANS UP (1926); SNOOKUMS DISAPPEARS (1926); SNOOKUMS' MERRY CHRISTMAS (1926); SNOOKUMS' OUTING (1926); SNOOKUMS' PLAY-MATES (1926); SNOOKUMS' TOOTH (1926); NEWLY-WEDS' ADVICE (1927); NEWLYWEDS' FALSE ALARM (1927); NEWLYWEDS' MISTAKE (1927); NEWLYWEDS' SERVANT (1927); NEWLYWEDS' SHOPPING TOUR (1927); NEWLYWEDS' SUCCESS (1927); NEWLYWEDS' SURPRISE (1927); NEWLYWEDS' TROUBLES (1927); SNOOKUMS ASLEEP (1927); STOP SNOOKUMS (1927); NEWLYWEDS' COURT TROUBLE (1928); NEWLYWEDS' HARD LUCK (1928); NEWLYWEDS LOSE SNOOKUMS (1928); NEWLYWEDS NEED HELP (1928); NEWLYWEDS UNWELCOME (1928); NEWLYWEDS' VISIT (1928); NEW-

LYWEDS CAMP OUT (1929); NEWLYWEDS' EXCUSE (1929); NEWLYWEDS' PESTS (1929).

This humor strip was created by George McManus for Pulitzer's *New York World* in 1904, and ran until it was discontinued in 1956. The strip related the endless misadventures of Mr. and Mrs. Newlywed and their spoiled-brat child Snookums. THE NEWLYWEDS strip was retitled THEIR ONLY CHILD when McManus moved to the Hearst Syndicate in 1912 where it ran until 1918. The strip was again retitled SNOOKUMS in 1944 until it was discontinued in 1956, two years after McManus' death. A series of live-action two-reel shorts based on the strip were produced for Universal Pictures by the Stern brothers. The directors of these silent shorts were, alternately, Gus Meins and Francis Corby. Mrs. Newlywed was played by Ethlyne Clair, and the obnoxious baby Snookums was played by child actor Sunny McKeen. The Snookums character was so popular that McKeen was featured in his own series of BABY SNOOKUMS shorts within the NEWLY-WEDS series, earning $15,000 a year by the time he was four years old.

OLD BILL
newspaper strip

OLD BILL AND SON (Legeran-GFD, 1940)—theatrical feature; 96 minutes.

Credits: Producers: Josef Somlo, Harold Boxall, Alexander Korda; Director: Ian Dalrymple; Screenplay: Bruce Bairnsfather, Arthur Wimperis, Ian Dalrymple (Based on Cartoons by Bruce Bairnsfather); Camera: Georges Perinal; Editor: Charles Crichton; Production Design: Vincent Korda; Music: Muir Mathieson.

Cast: Morland Graham (Old Bill Busby); John Mills (Young Bill Busby); Mary Clare (Maggie Busby); Renée Huston (Stella Malloy); René Ray (Sally); Gus McNaughton (Alf); Ronald Shiner (Bert); Janine Darcey (Françoise); Roland Culver (Colonel); Donald Stuart (Canuck); Manning Whiley (Chimp); Nicholas Phipps (Commentator); Allan Jeayes (Willoughby); Percy Walsh (Gustave).

OLD DOC YAK
newspaper strip

OLD DOC YAK—theatrical short subjects.

The following shorts were released by Selig-Polyscope Co.

OLD DOC YAK (1913); OLD DOC YAK AND THE ARTIST'S DREAM (1913); OLD DOC YAK'S CHRISTMAS (1913).

OLD DOC YAK, running from 1912 to 1919, was a funny-animal strip created by Sidney Smith for the *Chicago Tribune*, and related the misadventures of a humanized goat. The strip was briefly revived from 1930 to 1935. The three films based on the strip combined live-action and animation.

PEANUTS (CHARLIE BROWN)
newspaper strip

YOU'RE A GOOD MAN, CHARLIE BROWN (NBC, 1973)—TV special; 90 minutes; color.

Credits: Producers: Lee Mendelson, Warren L. Lockhart; Director: Walter C. Miller.

Cast: Wendell Burton (Charlie Brown); Ruby Persson (Lucy); Bill Hinnant (Snoopy); Mark Montgomery (Schroeder); Barry Livingston (Linus); Noelle Matlovsky (Peppermint Patty).

Note: This special was originally broadcast as a segment of *The Hallmark Hall of Fame.*

Cartoonist Charles Schulz created this hugely popular strip for United Features Syndicate in 1950, and the gentle humor of Schulz's characters has since been adapted in numerous television cartoon specials. The above TV special is the only live-action representation of Schulz's characters on film or tape, and was based on a Broadway musical.

THE PERILS OF GWENDOLINE
comic book

THE PERILS OF GWENDOLINE IN THE LAND OF THE YIK YAK (Samuel Goldwyn, 1984)—theatrical feature; 88 minutes; color.

Credits: Producers: Jean-Claude Eleury, Serge Laski; Director: Just Jaeckin; Screenplay: Just Jaeckin; Camera: André Domage; Music: Pierre Bachelet; Editor: Michelle Boehm; Designer: Françoise Deleu; Art Director: Andrew Guerin; Costumes: Daniel Elis; Sound: René Levert, Michelle Amsellem; Production Manager: Pierre Gauchet; Makeup: Reiko Kurk, Dominique Colladant.

Cast: Tawny Kitaen (Gwendoline); Brent Huff (Willard); Zabou (Beth); Bernadette Lafont (The Queen); Jean Rougerie (D'Arcy); Roland Amstutz; Jean Stanislas Capoul; Chen Chang Cheng; Vernon Dobtcheff; André Julien; Takashi Kawahara; Kristopher Kum; Loi Lam Duc; Maurice Lamy; Jim

Adhi Limas; Georges Lycan; Dominique Marcas; Roger Paschy; Hua Quach.

THE PHANTOM
newspaper strip

THE PHANTOM (Columbia, 1943)—theatrical serial; 15 chapters, first chapter approximately 30 minutes, remaining chapters approximately 20 minutes each.

Credits: Producer: Rudolph C. Flothow; Director: B. Reeves Eason; Screenplay: Morgan B. Cox, Victor McLeod, Sherman Lowe, Leslie J. Swabacker; Camera: James S. Brown, Jr.; Music: Lee Zahler; Editors: Dwight Caldwell, J. Henry Adams; Assistant Director: Richard Monroe.

Cast: Tom Tyler (The Phantom/Geoffrey Prescott); Jeanne Bates (Diana Palmer); Kenneth MacDonald (Dr. Bremmer); Frank Shannon (Professor Davidson); Guy Kingsford (Byron Andrews); Joe Devlin (Singapore Smith); Ernie Adams (Rusty); John S. Bagni (Moko); Ace, the Wonder Dog (Devil).

Chapter Titles: (1) The Sign of the Skull; (2) The Man Who Never Dies; (3) A Traitor's Code; (4) The Seat of Judgement; (5) The Ghost Who Walks; (6) Jungle Whispers; (7) The Mystery Well; (8) In Quest of the Keys; (9) The Fire Princess; (10) The Chamber of Death; (11) The Emerald Key; (12) The Fangs of the Beast; (13) The Road to Zoloz; (14) The Lost City; (15) Peace in the Jungle.

Created by writer Lee Falk and artist Ray Moore for King Features Syndicate, this jungle-adventure strip first appeared in February of 1936.

Falk's jungle hero was adapted to the screen by Columbia

THE PHANTOM (Columbia, 1943): Kenneth MacDonald, Tom Tyler, Frank Shannon, and Jeanne Bates in a publicity photo.

Pictures in 1943, with Tom Tyler (who also played Captain Marvel) in the lead. Although this serial is generally well made, it suffers from a hackneyed plot involving a search for a map that will lead to treasure buried in a lost city, and although Tyler was visually perfect for the role, his problems with dialogue were almost insurmountable, as was also the case with his performance in THE ADVENTURES OF CAPTAIN MARVEL. Both Tyler and no-talent Columbia starlet Jeanne Bates are nearly out-acted by Ace, the Wonder Dog, who portrays The Phantom's canine sidekick Devil with an aplomb that seems beyond Tyler and Bates. The real star of this serial, though, is heavy Kenneth MacDonald, whose thoroughly slimy (and frequently comical) villainy enlivened many a Three Stooges short. At one point, MacDonald confers with a member of The Phantom's expedition who, in a moment of greed, declares that he is willing to defect to MacDonald's party and ambush his former associates. "Well," oozes MacDonald, clearly admiring the malefactor's perfidy, "you've got possibilities!" It is one of the few shining moments in an otherwise lackluster film.

POPEYE
newspaper strip

POPEYE (Paramount, 1980)—theatrical feature; 114 minutes; color.

Credits: Producer: Robert Evans; Director: Robert Altman; Screenplay: Jules Feiffer; Camera: Giuseppe Rotummo; Music: Harry Nilsson; Editor: Tony Lombardo; Production Design: Wolf Kroeger; Costumes: Scott Bushnell; Choreography: Sharon Kinney; Hovey Burgess; Lou Wills.

Cast: Robin Williams (Popeye); Shelley Duvall (Olive Oyl); Ray Walston (Poopdeck Pappy); Paul L. Smith (Bluto); Paul Dooley (Wimpy); Richard Libertini (Geezil); Roberta Maxwell (Nana Oyl); Donald Moffat (Taxman); MacIntyre Dixon (Cole Oyl); Donovan Scott (Castor Oyl); Allan Nichols (Rough House); Wesley Ivan Hurt (Swee' Pea); Bill Irwin (Ham Gravy); Robert Fortier (Bill Barnacle, Town Drunk); David McCharen (Harry Hotcash, Gambler); Sharon Kinney (Cherry, His Moll); Peter Bray (Oxblood Oxheart, The Fighter); Linda Hunt (Mrs. Oxheart); Susan Kingsley (La Verne); Paul Zegler (Mayor Stonefeller); Pamela Burrell (Mrs. Stonefeller); Ray Cooper (Preacher); Geoff Hayle; Wayne Robson; Larry Pisoni; Carlo Pellegrini; Michael Christensen; Noel Parenti; Karen McCormick; John Bristol; Julie Janney; Patty Katz; Diane Shaffer; Nathalie Blossom; Dennis Franz; Carlos Brown; Ned Dowd; Hovey Burgess; Roberto Messina.

Created by Elsie Crisler Segar for the King Features Strip THIMBLE THEATRE, which began in December of 1919, and already included future supporting characters like Olive Oyl, the famed sailor man did not make his first appearance until January of 1929.

Popeye's most famous screen incarnation is, of course, in cartoon form, and the Max Fleischer shorts produced in the 1930s are some of the most entertaining cartoons ever made. The live-action musical directed by Robert Altman in 1980 was an ill-advised, miscalculated atrocity, and is a film that should be avoided at all costs. Although there are some decent sight gags in the film, star Robin Williams is hopelessly lost attempting to essay a role that is virtually impossible for a live actor to interpret, and the tacky quality of the production (despite a reported multimillion-dollar budget) and the mediocre "songs" hardly improved matters. There are some comic-strip characters that cannot be translated into flesh and blood, and the Robert Altman POPEYE proves this all too well.

PRINCE VALIANT
newspaper strip

PRINCE VALIANT (Twentieth Century-Fox, 1954)—theatrical feature; 100 minutes; color.

Credits: Producer: Robert L. Jacks; Director: Henry Hathaway; Screenplay: Dudley Nichols; Camera: Lucien Ballard; Music: Franz Waxman; Editor: Robert Simpson; Art Directors: Lyle Wheeler, Mark-Lee Kirk; Costumes: Charles Le Maire; Special Effects: Ray Kellogg.

Cast: James Mason (Sir Brack); Janet Leigh (Aleta); Robert Wagner (Prince Valiant); Sterling Hayden (Sir Gawain); Victor

McLaglen (Baltar); Donald Crisp (King Aguar); Brian Aherne (King Arthur); Barry Jones (King Luke); Mary Philips (Queen); Howard Wendell (Morgan Todd); Tom Conway (Sir Kay); Sammy Ogg (Small Page); Neville Brand (Viking Warrior Chief); Ben Wright (Seneschol); Jarma Lewis (Queen Guinevere); Robert Adler (Sir Brack's Man-at-Arms); Ray Spiker (Gorlock); Primo Carnera (Sligon); Basil Ruysdael (Old Viking); Fortune Gordon (Strangler); Percival Vivian (Doctor); Don Megowan (Sir Lancelot); Richard Webb (Sir Galahad); John Dierkes (Sir Tristram); Carleton Young (Herald); Otto Waldis (Patch Eye); John Davidson (Patriarch); Lloyd Aherne, Jr. (Prince Valiant, Age 12); Lou Nova (Captain of the Guards); Hal Baylor, Mickey Simpson (Prison Guards); Eugene Roth (Viking).

Created by Harold ("Hal") Foster for King Features Syndicate, this famous medieval-adventure strip first appeared in February of 1937. Foster's strip gained justifiable repute for its fine artwork, attention to detail and historical accuracy. The film adaptation was a bit stolid in pace and style, and was hampered somewhat by the casting of Robert Wagner in the title role, but benefitted greatly from top-of-the-line production values and lush Technicolor photography.

RADIO PATROL
newspaper strip

RADIO PATROL (Universal, 1937)—theatrical serial; 12 chapters, each chapter approximately 20 minutes.

Credits: Associate Producers: Barney A. Sarecky, Ben Koenig; Directors: Ford Beebe, Cliff Smith; Screenplay: Norman S. Hall, Wyndham Gittens, Ray Trampe; Camera: Jerry Ash;

Supervising Editor: Saul A. Goodkind; Editors: Alvin Todd, Louis Sackin, Joe Gluck; Art Director: Ralph DeLacy.

Cast: Grant Withers (Pat O'Hara); Catherine Hughes (Molly); Mickey Rentschler (Pinky Adams); Adrian Morris (Sam); Max Hoffman, Jr. (Selkirk); Frank Lackteen (Thata); Leonard Lord (Franklin); Monte Montague (Pollard); Dick Botiller (Zutta); Silver Wolf (Irish).

Chapter Titles: (1) A Million Dollar Murder; (2) The Hypnotic Eye; (3) Flaming Death; (4) The Human Clue; (5) The Flash of Doom; (6) The House of Terror; (7) Claws of Steel; (8) The Perfect Crime; (9) Plaything of Disaster; (10) A Bargain With Death; (11) The Hidden Menace; (12) They Get Their Man.

Created by Eddie Sullivan and Charles Schmidt, this police-adventure strip (the original title was PINKERTON, JR.) was distributed by King Features Syndicate from April of 1934 until it was discontinued in December of 1950.

RED BARRY
newspaper strip

RED BARRY (Universal, 1938)—theatrical serial; 13 chapters, each chapter approximately 20 minutes.

Credits: Associate Producer: Barney A. Sarecky; Directors: Ford Beebe, Alan James; Screenplay: Norman S. Hall, Ray Trampe; Camera: Jerry Ash; Art Director: Ralph DeLacy; Music: Charles Previn; Editors: Saul A. Goodkind, Alvin Todd, Louis Sackin; Sound: Bernard B. Brown; Technician: Jesse A. Moulin.

Cast: Larry "Buster" Crabbe (Red Barry); Frances Robinson (Mississippi); Edna Sedgewick (Natacha); Cyril Delevanti (Wing Fu); Frank Lackteen (Quong Fu); Wade Boteler (Inspector Scott); Hugh Huntley (Vane); Philip Ahn (Cholly); William Ruhl (Mannix); William Gould (Commissioner); Wheeler Oakman (Weaver); Stanley Price (Petrov); Earle Douglas (Igor); Charles Stevens (Captain Moy).

Chapter Titles: (1) Millions for Defense; (2) The Curtain Falls; (3) The Decoy; (4) High Stakes; (5) Desperate Chances; (6) The Human Target; (7) Midnight Tragedy; (8) The Devil's Disguise; (9) Between Two Fires; (10) The False Trail; (11) Heavy Odds; (12) The Enemy Within; (13) Mission of Mercy.

This rather exotic crime-adventure strip, about an undercover policeman stationed in Chinatown, was created by Will Gould for King Features Syndicate, and ran from March of 1934 until 1940.

RED RYDER
newspaper strip

ADVENTURES OF RED RYDER (Republic, 1940)— theatrical serial; 12 chapters, first chapter approximately 30 minutes, remaining chapters approximately 20 minutes each.

Credits: Associate Producer: Hiram S. Brown, Jr.; Directors: William Witney, John English; Screenplay: Ronald Davidson, Franklyn Adreon, Sol Shor, Barney Sarecky, Norman S. Hall; Camera: William Nobles; Music: Cy Feuer.

Cast: Don "Red" Barry (Red Ryder); Noah Beery (Ace Hanlon); Tommy Cook (Little Beaver); Bob Kortman (One

ADVENTURES OF RED RYDER (Republic, 1940): Tommy Cook and Don "Red" Barry, *center.*

Eye); William Farnum (Col. Tom Ryder); Maude Pierce Allen (Duchess); Vivian Coe (Beth); Hal Taliaferro (Cherokee); Harry Worth (Calvin Drake); Carleton Young (Sheriff Dade); Ray Teal (Shark); Gene Alsace (Deputy Lawson); Gayne Whitman (Harrison); Hooper Atchley (Treadway); John Dilson (Hale); Lloyd Ingraham (Sheriff Andrews); Charles Hutchinson (Rancher Brown); Gardner James (Barnett); Wheaton Chambers (Boswell); Lynton Brent (Clark).

Chapter Titles: (1) Murder on the Santa Fe Trail; (2) Horsemen of Death; (3) Trail's End; (4) Water Rustlers; (5) Avalanche; (6) Hangman's Noose; (7) Framed; (8) Blazing Walls; (9) Records of Doom; (10) One Second to Live; (11) The Devil's Marksman; (12) Frontier Justice.

CHEYENNE WILDCAT (Republic, 1944)—theatrical feature; 56 minutes.

Credits: Associate Producer: Louis Gray; Director: Lesley Selander; Screenplay: Randall Faye.

Cast: Bill Elliott; Bobby Blake; Alice Fleming; Peggy Stewart; Francis McDonald; Roy Barcroft; Tom London; Tom Chatterton; Kenne Duncan; Bud Geary; Jack Kirk; Sam Burton; Bud Osborne; Bob Wilke; Rex Lease; Tom Steele; Charles Morton; Forrest Taylor; Franklyn Farnum; Wee Willie Keller; Universal Jack; Tom Smith; Rudy Bowman; Horace B. Carpenter; Frank Ellis; Steve Clark; Bob Burns; Jack O'Shea.

MARSHAL OF RENO (Republic, 1944)—theatrical feature; 54 minutes.

Credits: Associate Producer: Louis Gray; Director: Wallace Grissell; Screenplay: Anthony Coldeway (Original Story: Anthony Coldeway, Taylor Cavan).

Cast: Bill Elliott; George Hayes; Bobby Blake; Alice Fleming; Herbert Rawlinson; Tom London; Jay Kirby; Charles King; Jack Kirk; Kenne Duncan; Leroy Mason; Bob Wilke; Fred Burns; Tom Steele; Edmund Cobb; Fred Graham; Blake Edwards; Hal Price; Bud Geary; Jack O'Shea; Al Taylor; Marshall Reed; Tom Chatterton; Carl Sepulveda; Ken Terrell; Horace B. Carpenter; Charles Sullivan; Roy Barcroft.

THE SAN ANTONIO KID (Republic, 1944)—theatrical feature; 59 minutes.

Credits: Associate Producer: Stephen Auer; Director: Howard Bretherton; Screenplay: Norman S. Hall.

Cast: Bill Elliott; Bobby Blake; Alice Fleming; Linda Stirling; Tom London; Earle Hodgins; Glenn Strange; Duncan Renaldo; Leroy Mason; Jack Kirk; Bob Wicke; Cliff Parkinson; Jack O'Shea; Tex Terry; Bob Woodward; Herman Hack; Henry Wills; Tom Steele; Joe Garcia; Billy Vincent; Bud Geary.

THE SHERIFF OF LAS VEGAS (Republic, 1944)—theatrical feature; 55 minutes.

Credits: Associate Producer: Stephen Auer; Director: Lesley Selander; Screenplay: Norman S. Hall.

Cast: Bill Elliott; Bobby Blake; Alice Fleming; Peggy Stewart; Selmer Jackson; William Haade; Jay Kirby; John Hamilton; Kenne Duncan; Bud Geary; Jack Kirk; Dickie Dillon; Frank McCarroll; Freddie Chapman.

TUCSON RAIDERS (Republic, 1944)—theatrical feature; 55 minutes.

Credits: Associate Producer: Eddy White; Director: Spencer G. Bennett; Screenplay: Anthony Coldeway (Original Story: Jack O'Donnell).

Cast: Bill Elliott; George Hayes; Bobby Blake; Alice Fleming; Ruth Lee; Peggy Stewart; Leroy Mason; Stanley Andrews; John Whitney; Bud Geary; Karl Hackett; Tom Steele; Tom Chatterton; Edward Cassidy; Edward Howard; Fred Graham; Frank McCarroll; Marshall Reed; Frank Pershing; Roy Barcroft; Kenne Duncan; Tom London; Jack Kirk.

VIGILANTES OF DODGE CITY (Republic, 1944)— theatrical feature; 54 minutes.

Credits: Associate Producer: Stephen Auer; Director: Wallace Grissell; Screenplay: Norman S. Hall, Anthony Coldeway.

Cast: Bill Elliott; Bobby Blake; Alice Fleming; Linda Stirling; Leroy Mason; Hal Taliaferro; Tom London; Stephen Barclay; Bud Geary; Kenne Duncan; Bob Wilke; Horace B. Carpenter; Stanley Andrews.

COLORADO PIONEERS (Republic, 1945)—theatrical feature; 57 minutes.

Credits: Associate Producer: Sidney Picker; Director: R. G. Springsteen; Screenplay: Earle Snell (Original Story: Peter Whitehead).

Cast: Bill Elliott; Bobby Blake; Alice Fleming; Roy Barcroft; Bud Geary; Billy Cummings; Freddie Chapman; Frank Jacquet; Tom London; Monte Hale; Buckwheat Thomas; George Chesebro; Emmett Vogan; Tom Chatterton; Edward Cassidy; Fred Graham; Cliff Parkinson; Horace B. Carpenter; Bill Wolfe; Jess Cavin; Howard Mitchell; Jack Rockwell; George Morrell; Jack Kirk; Gary Armstrong; Bobby Anderson; Roger Williams; Richard Lydon; Robert Goldschmidt; Romey Foley.

THE GREAT STAGECOACH ROBBERY (Republic, 1945)—theatrical feature; 56 minutes.

Credits: Associate Producer: Louis Gray; Director: Lesley Selander; Screenplay: Randall Faye.

Cast: Bill Elliott; Bobby Blake; Alice Fleming; Francis McDonald; Don Costello; Sylvia Arslan; Bud Geary; Leon Tyler; Freddie Chapman; Henry Wills; Hank Bell; Bob Wilke; John James; Tom London; Dickie Dillon; Bobby Dillon; Raymond

ZeBrack; Patsy May; Chris Wren; Horace Carpenter; Frederick Howard.

LONE TEXAS RANGER (Republic, 1945)—theatrical feature; 56 minutes.

Credits: Associate Producer: Louis Gray; Director: Spencer Bennet; Screenplay: Bob Williams.

Cast: Bill Elliott; Bobby Blake; Alice Fleming; Roy Barcroft; Helen Talbot; Jack McClendon; Rex Lease; Tom Chatterton; Jack Kirk; Nelson McDowell; Larry Olson; Dale Van Sickle; Frank O'Connor; Bob Wilke; Bud Geary; Budd Buster; Hal Price; Horace B. Carpenter; Nolan Leary; Tom Steele; Leroy Mason; Earl Dobbins; Bill Stevens.

MARSHAL OF LAREDO (Republic, 1945)—theatrical feature; 56 minutes.

Credits: Associate Producer: Sidney Picker; Director: R. G. Springsteen; Screenplay: Bob Williams.

Cast: Bill Elliott; Bobby Blake; Alice Fleming; Peggy Stewart; Roy Barcroft; Tom London; George Carleton; Wheaton Chambers; Tom Chatterton; George Chesebro; Don Costello; Bud Geary; Robert Grady; Sarah Padden; Jack O'Shea; Lane Bradford; Ken Terrell; Dorothy Granger; Dick Scott.

PHANTOM OF THE PLAINS (Republic, 1945)—theatrical feature; 56 minutes.

Credits: Associate Producer: R. G. Springsteen; Director: Lesley Selander; Screenplay: Earle Snell, Charles Kenyon.

Cast: Bill Elliott; Bobby Blake; Alice Fleming; Ian Keith; William Haade; Virginia Christine; Bud Geary; Henry Hall; Fred Graham; Jack Kirk; Jack Rockwell; Tom London; Earle Hodgins; Rose Plummer.

WAGON WHEELS WESTWARD (Republic, 1945)— theatrical feature; 56 minutes.

Credits: Associate Producer: Sidney Picker; Director; R. G. Springsteen; Screenplay: Earle Snell (Original Story: Gerald Geraghty).

Cast: Bill Elliott; Bobby Blake; Alice Fleming; Linda Stirling; Roy Barcroft; Emmett Lynn; Jay Kirby; Dick Curtis; George J. Lewis; Bud Geary; Tom London; Kenne Duncan; George Chesebro; Tom Chatterton; Frank Ellis; Bob McKenzie; Jack Kirk.

CALIFORNIA GOLD RUSH (Republic, 1946)—theatrical feature; 51 minutes.

Credits: Associate Producer: Sidney Picker; Director: R. G. Springsteen; Screenplay: Bob Williams.

Cast: Bill Elliott; Bobby Blake; Alice Fleming; Peggy Stewart; Russell Simpson; Dick Curtis; Joel Friedkin; Kenne Duncan; Monte Hale; Tom London; Wen Wright; Dickie Dillon; Jack Kirk; Mary Arden; Budd Buster; Bud Osborne; Neal Hart; Frank Ellis; Jim Mitchell; Herman Hack; Freddie Chapman; Jess Cavan; Pascale Perry; Silver Harr.

CONQUEST OF CHEYENNE (Republic, 1946)—theatrical feature; 55 minutes.

Credits: Associate Producer: Walter Wanger; Director; R. G. Springsteen; Screenplay: Ernest Pascal (Original Story: Ernest Haycox).

Cast: Bill Elliott; Bobby Blake; Alice Fleming; Peggy Stewart; Jay Kirby; Milton Kibbee; Tom London; Emmett Lynn; Kenne Duncan; George Sherwood; Frank McCarroll; Jack Kirk; Tom Chatterton; Ted Mapes; Jack Rockwell.

SANTA FE UPRISING (Republic, 1946)—theatrical feature; 55 minutes.

Credits: Associate Producer: Sidney Picker; Director: R. G. Springsteen; Screenplay: Earle Snell.

Cast: Allan Lane; Bobby Blake; Martha Wentworth; Barton MacLane; Jack LaRue; Tom London; Dick Curtis; Forrest Taylor; Emmett Lynn; Hank Patterson; Edmund Cobb; Pat Michaels; Kenne Duncan; Edythe Elliott; Frank Ellis; Art Dillard; Lee Reynolds; Forrest Burns.

SHERIFF OF REDWOOD VALLEY (Republic, 1946)—theatrical feature; 54 minutes.

Credits: Associate Producer: Sidney Picker; Director: R. G. Springsteen; Screenplay: Earle Snell.

Cast: Bill Elliott; Bobby Blake; Alice Fleming; Bob Steele; Peggy Stewart; Arthur Loft; James Craven; Tom London; Kenne Duncan; Bud Geary; John Wayne Wright; Tom Chatterton; Budd Buster; Frank McCarroll; Frank Linn.

STAGECOACH TO DENVER (Republic, 1946)—theatrical feature; 56 minutes.

Credits: Associate Producer: Sidney Picker; Director: R. G. Springsteen; Screenplay: Earle Snell.

Cast: Allan Lane; Bobby Blake; Martha Wentworth; Peggy Stewart; Roy Barcroft; Emmett Lynn; Ted Adams; Edmund Cobb; Tom Chatterton; Bobbie Hyatt; George Chesebro; Edward Cassidy; Wheaton Chambers; Forrest Taylor; Britt Wood; Tom London; Stanley Price.

SUN VALLEY CYCLONE (Republic, 1946)—theatrical feature; 56 minutes.

Credits: Associate Producer: Sidney Picker; Director: R. G. Springsteen; Screenplay: Earle Snell.

Cast: Bill Elliott; Bobby Blake; Alice Fleming; Roy Barcroft; Monte Hale; Kenne Duncan; Eddy Waller; Tom London; Edmund Cobb; Edward Cassidy; George Chesebro; Rex Lease; Hal Price; Jack Kirk; Frank O'Connor; Jack Sparks.

HOMESTEADERS OF PARADISE VALLEY (Republic, 1947)—theatrical feature; 59 minutes.

Credits: Associate Producer: Sidney Picker; Director: R. G. Springsteen; Screenplay: Earle Snell.

Cast: Allan Lane; Bobby Blake; Martha Wentworth; Ann Todd; Gene Stutenroth; John James; Mauritz Hugo; Emmett Vogan; Milton Kibbee; Tom London; Edythe Elliott; George Chesebro; Edward Cassidy; Jack Kirk; Herman Hack.

THE MARSHAL OF CRIPPLE CREEK (Republic, 1947)—theatrical feature; 58 minutes.

Credits: Associate Producer: Sidney Picker; Director: R. G. Springsteen; Screenplay: Earle Snell.

Cast: Allan Lane; Bobby Blake; Martha Wentworth; Trevor Bardette; Tom London; Roy Barcroft; Gene Stutenroth; William Self; Helen Wallace.

OREGON TRAIL SCOUTS (Republic, 1947)—theatrical feature; 58 minutes.

Credits: Associate Producer: Sidney Picker; Director: R. G. Springsteen; Screenplay: Earle Snell.

Cast: Allan Lane; Bobby Blake; Martha Wentworth; Roy Barcroft; Emmett Lynn; Edmund Cobb; Earle Hodgins; Edward Cassidy; Frank Lackteen; Billy Cummings; Jack Kirk; Jack O'Shea; Chief Yowlachie.

RUSTLERS OF DEVIL'S CANYON (Republic, 1947)—theatrical feature; 58 minutes.

Credits: Associate Producer: Sidney Picker; Director: R. G. Springsteen; Screenplay: Earle Snell.

Cast: Allan Lane; Bobby Blake; Martha Wentworth; Peggy Stewart; Arthur Space; Emmett Lynn; Roy Barcroft; Tom London; Harry Carr; Pierce Lyden; Forrest Taylor; Bob Burns.

VIGILANTES OF BOOMTOWN (Republic, 1947)—theatrical feature; 56 minutes.

Credits: Associate Producer: Sidney Picker; Director: R. G. Springsteen; Screenplay: Earle Snell.

Cast: Allan Lane; Bobby Blake, Martha Wentworth; Roy Barcroft; Peggy Stewart; George Turner; Eddie Lou Simms; George Chesebro; Bobby Barber; George Lloyd; Ted Adams; John Dehner; Earle Hodgins; Harlan Briggs; Budd Buster; Jack O'Shea; Tom Steele.

THE COWBOY AND THE PRIZEFIGHTER (Equity/Eagle Lion, 1949)—theatrical feature; 59 minutes; color.

Credits: Producer: Jerry Thomas; Director: Lewis D. Collins; Screenplay: Jerry Thomas.

Cast: Jim Bannon; Don Kay Reynolds; Emmett Lynn; Marin Sais; Lou Nova; Don Haggerty; Karen Randle; John Hart; Marshall Reed; Forrest Taylor; Lane Bradford; Bud Osborne; Steve Clark; Ray Jones.

THE FIGHTING REDHEAD (Equity/Eagle Lion, 1949)— theatrical feature; 55 minutes; color.

Credits: Producer: Jerry Thomas; Director: Lewis D. Collins; Screenplay: Paul Franklin, Jerry Thomas.

Cast: Jim Bannon; Don Kay Reynolds; Emmett Lynn; Marin Sais; Peggy Stewart; John Hart; Lane Bradford; Forrest Taylor; Lee Roberts; Bob Duncan; Sandy Sanders; Billy Hammond; Ray Jones.

RIDE, RYDER, RIDE (Equity/Eagle Lion, 1949)—theatrical feature; 60 minutes; color.

Credits: Producer: Jerry Thomas; Director: Lewis D. Collins; Screenplay: Paul Franklin.

Cast: Jim Bannon; Don Kay Reynolds; Emmett Lynn; Peggy Stewart; Gaylord Pendleton; Jack O'Shea; Jean Budinger; Marin Sais; Stanley Blystone; William Fawcett; Billy Hammond; Edwin Max; Steve Clark.

ROLL, THUNDER, ROLL (Equity/Eagle Lion, 1949)—theatrical feature; 60 minutes; color.

Credits: Producer: Jerry Thomas; Director: Lewis D. Collins; Screenplay: Jerry Thomas.

Cast: Jim Bannon; Don Kay Reynolds; Emmett Lynn; Marin Sais; Glenn Strange; Nancy Gates; I. Stanford Jolley; Lee Morgan; Lane Bradford; Steven Pendleton; Charles Stevens; William Fawcett; Dorothy Latta; Joe Green; Rocky Shahan; Carol Henry; George Chesebro; Jack O'Shea.

RED RYDER (Syndicated, 1956)—TV series; 39 episodes, 30 minutes each.

Cast: Rocky Lane (Red Ryder); Louis Letteri (Little Beaver); Elizabeth Slifer (The Duchess).

This western hero was created by Fred Harman for the NEA Service, and ran from November of 1938 until the late 1960s.

THE SAD SACK
newspaper strip

THE SAD SACK (Paramount, 1957)—theatrical feature; 98 minutes.

Credits: Producer: Hal B. Wallis; Director: George Marshall; Screenplay: Edmund Beloin, Nate Monaster; Camera: Loyal Griggs; Music: Walter Scharf; Editor: Archie Marshek; Art Directors: Hal Pereira, John Goodman; Costumes: Edith Head; Choreography: Charles O'Curron; Music and Lyrics (for the song "The Sad Sack"): Hal David, Burt F. Bacharach.

Cast: Jerry Lewis (Bixby); David Wayne (Dolan); Phyllis Kirk (Major Shelton); Peter Lorre (Abdul); Joe Mantell (Pvt. Stan Wenaslawsky); Gene Evens (Sergeant Pulley); George Dolenz (Ali Mustapha); Liliane Montevecchi (Zita); Shepperd Strudwick (General Vanderlip); Abraham Sofaer (Hassim); Mary Treen (Sergeant Hansen); Drew Cahill (Lieutenant Wilson); Michael G. Ansara (Moki); Don Haggerty (Captain Ward); Jean Del Val (French General); Dan Seymour (Arab Chieftain); Yvette Vickers (Hazel).

This simplistic army-humor strip was created by ex-Disney animator George Baker in 1942 for the U.S. Army weekly *Yank Magazine,* and was picked up for newspaper distribution by the Bell Syndicate in May of 1946. The strip was discontinued in the early 1950s, but comic book adaptations, drawn by other hands (with Baker drawing the covers), carried on. The Jerry Lewis film is an adaptation in name only and is, predictably, merely an egocentric showcase for Lewis' usual tiresome nonsense, with true professionals like Peter Lorre helplessly trapped in the morass.

THE SEA HOUND
comic book
Avon Periodicals

THE SEA HOUND (Columbia, 1947)—theatrical serial; 15 chapters, first chapter approximately 30 minutes, remaining chapters approximately 20 minutes each.

Credits: Sam Katzman; Directors: Walter B. Eason, Mack Wright; Screenplay: George H. Plympton, Lewis Clay, Arthur Hoerl; Camera: Ira H. Morgan; Music: Mischa Bakaleinikoff; Editor: Earl Turner; Assistant Director: Mack Wright.

Cast: Buster Crabbe (Captain Silver); James Lloyd (Tex); Pamela Blake (Ann Whitney); Ralph Hodges (Jerry); Spencer Chan ("Cookie" Kukai); Robert Barron (Admiral); Hugh Prosser (Stanley Rand); Rick Vallin (Manilla Pete); Jack Ingram (Murdock); Milton Kibbee (John Whitney); Al Baffert (Lon); Stanley Blystone (Black Mike); Robert Duncan (Sloan); Pierce Lyden (Vardman); Rusty Wescoatt (Singapore Manson); Emmett Lynn (Van Wart); William Fawcett (André).

Chapter Titles: (1) Captain Silver Sails Again; (2) Spanish Gold; (3) The Mystery of the Map; (4) Menaced by Ryaks; (5) Captain Silver's Strategy; (6) The Sea Hound at Bay; (7) In the Admiral's Lair; (8) Rand's Treachery; (9) On the Water Wheel; (10) On the Treasure Trail; (11) The Sea Hound Attacked; (12) Dangerous Waters; (13) The Panther's Prey; (14) The Fatal Doublecross; (15) Captain Silver's Last Stand.

This seafaring adventure character first appeared in CAPTAIN SILVER'S LOG OF THE SEA HOUND #1 in 1945.

SECRET AGENT X–9
newspaper strip

SECRET AGENT X–9 (Universal, 1937)—theatrical serial; 12 chapters, each chapter approximately 20 minutes.

Credits: Directors: Forde Beebe, Cliff Smith; Screenplay: Wyndham Gittens, Norman S. Hall, Ray Trampe, Leslie Swabacker.

Cast: Scott Kolk (Secret Agent X–9); Jean Rogers (Shara Graustark); Henry Hunter (Tommy Dawson); David Oliver (Pidge); Larry Blake (Wheeler); Monte Blue (Baron Michael Karsten); Henry Brandon (Blackstone/Brenda); Lon Chaney, Jr. (Maroni); Max Hoffman, Jr. (Marker); Bentley Hewlett (Scarlett); George Shelley (Packard); Robert Dalton (Thurston); Leonard Lord (Ransom); Bob Kortman (Trader DeLaney); Edward Piel, Sr. (The Fence); Lynn Gilbert (Rose).

Chapter Titles: (1) Modern Pirates; (2) The Ray That Blinds; (3) The Man of Many Faces; (4) The Listening Shadow; (5) False Fires; (6) The Dragnet; (7) Sealed Lips; (8) Exhibit A; (9) The Masquerader; (10) The Forced Lie; (11) The Enemy Camp; (12) Crime Does Not Pay.

SECRET AGENT X–9 (Universal, 1945)—theatrical serial; 13 chapters, each chapter approximately 20 minutes.

Credits: Directors: Ray Taylor, Lewis D. Collins; Screenplay: Joseph O'Donnell, Patricia Harper (Original Story: Joseph O'Donnell, Harold C. Wire).

Cast: Lloyd Bridges (Secret Agent X–9); Keye Luke (Ah Fong); Jan Wiley (Lynn Moore); Victoria Horne (Nabura); Samuel S. Hinds (Solo); Cy Kendall (Lucky Number); Jack Overman (Marker); George Lynn (Bach); Clarence Lang (Takahari); Benson Fong (Hakahima); Arno Frey (Kapitan Graf); Gene Stutenroth (Yogel); Ann Codee (Mama Pierrie); Edward M. Howard (Drag Dorgan); Edmund Cobb (Bartender).

Chapter Titles: (1) Torpedo Rendezvous; (2) Ringed By Fire; (3) Death Curve; (4) Floodlight Murder; (5) Doom Downgrade; (6) Strafed By a Zero; (7) High Pressure Deadline; (8) The Dropping Floor; (9) The Danger Point; (10) Japanese Burial;

(11) Fireworks for Dead Men; (12) Big Gun Fusillade; (13) Zero Minute.

This secret agent–adventure strip was created by Alex Raymond for King Features Syndicate and first appeared in January of 1934. The first four entries were written by none other than famed mystery author Dashiell Hammett, who left his distinctive mark on the strip, and succeeding writers included Leslie Charteris, creator of "The Saint."

SHEENA
comic book
Fiction House

SHEENA, QUEEN OF THE JUNGLE (Syndicated, 1955)— TV series; 26 episodes, 30 minutes each.

Credits: Executive Producers: Don Sharpe, William Nassour; Producer: Edward Nassour.

Cast: Irish McCalla (Sheena); Christian Drake (Bob).

SHEENA (Columbia, 1984)—theatrical feature; 117 minutes; color.

Credits: Executive Producer: Yoram Ben-Ami; Producer: Paul Aratow; Director: John Guillerman; Screenplay: David Newman, Lorenzo Semple, Jr. (Original Story: David Newman, Leslie Stevens); Camera: Pasqualino De Santis; Editor: Ray Lovejoy; Music: Richard Hartley; Production Design: Peter Murton; Art Director: Malcolm Middleton; Set Decorator: Ian Watson; Costumes: Annalista Nasalli-Rocca; Sound: Brian

SHEENA, QUEEN OF THE JUNGLE (1955): Irish McCalla in the syndicated TV series.

Simmons; Special Effects Supervisor: Peter Hutchinson; Special Effects Coordinator: Bob Nugent; Animal Trainer: Hubert G. Wells; Associate Producers: Christian Ferry, Alan Rinzler.

Cast: Tanya Roberts (Sheena); Ted Wass (Vic Casey); Donovan Scott (Fletcher); Elizabeth Of Toro (Shaman); France Zobda (Countess Zanda); Trevor Thomas (Prince Otwani); Clifton Jones (King Jabalani); John Forgeham (Jorgensen); Errol John

(Bolu); Sylvester Williams (Juka); Bob Sherman (Grizzard); Michael Shannon (Philip Ames); Nancy Paul (Betsy Ames); Kathryn Grant (Child Sheena); Kirsty Lindsay (Young Sheena).

Created by writer S. M. Iger and artist Will Eisner for the Editor's Press Service in 1937, this shapely female version of Tarzan was eventually adapted to comic books, making her first book appearance in JUMBO #1 in September of 1938, running until the March 1953 issue.

Sheena's television incarnation in the person of actress Irish McCalla remains the most fondly remembered adaptation of the character, while a recent feature-film version starring lovely but vapid Tanya Roberts is already forgotten.

SKIPPY
newspaper strip

SKIPPY (Paramount, 1931)—theatrical feature; 85 minutes.

Credits: Producer: Louis D. Lighton; Director: Norman Taurog; Screenplay: Joseph L. Mankiewicz, Norman McLeod, Don Marquis, Percy Crosby, Sam Mintz; Camera: Karl Struss.

Cast: Jackie Cooper (Skippy Skinner); Robert Coogan (Sooky Wayne); Mitzie Green (Eloise); Jackie Searle (Sidney); Willard Robertson (Dr. Herbert Skinner); David Haines (Harley Nubbins); Helen Jerome Eddy (Mrs. Wayne); Jack Clifford (Dogcatcher Nubbins); Guy Oliver (Dad Burkey).

SOOKY (Paramount, 1931)—theatrical feature; 85 minutes.

Credits: Director: Norman Taurog; Screenplay: Sam Mintz, Joseph L. Mankiewicz, Norman McLeod; Camera: Arthur Todd.

Cast: Jackie Searl (Sidney Saunders); Willard Robertson (Mr. Skinner); Enid Bennett (Mrs. Skinner); Helen Jerome Eddy (Mrs. Wayne); Leigh Allen (Mr. Saunders); Harry Beresford (Mr. Willoughby); Jackie Cooper (Skippy Skinner); Robert Coogan (Sooky Wayne); Oscar Apfel (Krausmyer); Guy Oliver (Mr. Moggs); Gertrude Sutton (Hilda); Tom Wilson.

This children's humor strip (very much in the same mold as Charles Schulz' PEANUTS) was created by Percy Crosby for *Life Humor* magazine in 1919. The strip was picked up for newspaper distribution by King Features Syndicate in 1928, although Crosby retained ownership. SKIPPY ran until Crosby, overcome by illness, finally withdrew the strip in 1943.

The Paramount film based on the strip, SKIPPY, earned its director, Norman Taurog, the Oscar for best direction.

SMILIN' JACK
newspaper strip

ADVENTURES OF SMILIN' JACK (Universal, 1942)— theatrical serial; 13 chapters, each chapter approximately 20 minutes.

Credits: Producer: Ford Beebe; Associate Producer: Donald H. Brown; Directors: Ray Taylor, Lewis D. Collins; Screenplay: Morgan B. Cox; Camera: William Sickner; Art Director: H. H. MacArthur; Music: H. J. Salter; Supervising Editor: Saul A. Goodkind; Editors: Al Todd, Louis Sackin, Edgar Zane, Irving Birmbaum; Sound: Bernard B. Brown; Technician: Charles C. Carroll; Dialogue Director: Jacques Jaccard.

Cast: Tom Brown (Jack Martin); Rose Hobart (Fräulein Von Teufel); Marjorie Lord (Janet); Philip Ahn (Wu Tan); Jay Novello (Kushimi); Nigel de Brulier (Lo San); Edgar Barrier

(Tommy); Turhan Bey (Kageyama); Keye Luke (Captain Wing); Sidney Toler (General Kai Ling); Cyril Delavanti (Mah Ling); Rico De Montez.

Chapter Titles: (1) The High Road to Doom; (2) The Rising Sun Strikes; (3) Attacked by Bombers; (4) Knives of Vengeance; (5) A Watery Grave; (6) Escape by Clipper; (7) Fifteen Fathoms Below; (8) Treachery at Sea; (9) The Bridge of Peril; (10) Blackout in the Islands; (11) Held for Treason; (12) The Torture Fire Test; (13) Sinking the Rising Sun.

This aviation-adventure strip was created by Zack Mosley (the original title was ON THE WING) for the Chicago Tribune-New York News Syndicate, and ran from 1933 to 1973. The Universal serial based on the strip was one of the studio's best chapterplays, and was also the last Universal serial based on a comic-strip character.

SPIDER-MAN
comic book
Marvel Comics

THE ELECTRIC COMPANY (PBS, 1971–76)—TV series; each episode 30 minutes; color.

Notes: Spider-Man was portrayed by a live actor in various instructional sketches on this children's educational series.

SPIDER-MAN (CBS, 1977)—TV movie; 90 minutes; color.

Credits: Producer: Edward J. Montague; Director: E. W. Swackhamer; Screenplay: Alvin Boretz; Camera: Fred Jackman; Art Director: James Hulsey; Music: Johnnie Spence.

THE AMAZING SPIDER-MAN (CBS-TV, 1978): A tackily garbed Nicholas Hammond (or his stunt double) in the title role.

Cast: Nicholas Hammond (Spider-Man/Peter Parker); David White (J. Jonah Jameson); Michael Pataki (Captain Barbera); Hilly Hicks (Robbie Robinson); Lisa Eilbacher (Judy Tyler); Jeff Donnell (May Parker); Bob Hastings (Monihan); Ivor Francis (Noah Tyler); Thayer David (Edward Byron); Dick Balduzzi (Delivery Man); Barry Cutler (Purse Snatcher).

THE AMAZING SPIDER-MAN (CBS, 1978–79)—TV series; 12 episodes, 60 minues each; color.

Credits: Executive Producers: Charles Fries, Daniel R. Goodman; Producers: Robert Janes, Ron Satlof, Lionel E. Siegel; Series Directors: Ron Satlof, Michael Caffey, Fernando Lamas, Dennis Donnelly, Cliff Bole, Larry Stewart, Tom Blank, Joseph Manduke; Series Writers: Robert Janes, John Bloch, B. W. Sandefur, Lionel E. Siegel; Music: Stu Phillips, Dana Kaproff; Stunts: Fred Waugh.

Cast: Nicholas Hammond (Spider-Man/Peter Parker); Robert F. Simon (J. Jonah Jameson); Michael Pataki (Captain Barbera); Chip Fields (Rita Conway); Ellen Bry (Julie Masters); Irene Tedrow (Aunt May).

Created by writer-editor Stan Lee and artist Steve Ditko, SPIDER-MAN first appeared in AMAZING FANTASY #15 in August of 1962, and the immediately popular strip was quickly given its own book.

Stan Lee and his stable of artists revitalized the comic-book industry in the 1960s by creating more complex heroic figures, or, as Lee himself once phrased it, "superheroes with problems." Marvel characters like SPIDER-MAN and THE FANTASTIC FOUR were immediately successful with a new generation of comic-book readers, and the Marvel characters made their veteran rivals, Superman and Batman seem tired and played out by comparison. Lee, working with his main artists Jack Kirby and Steve Ditko, created a comic-book revolution, and in retrospect it seems odd that Hollywood took so long to realize the potential of the Marvel characters, and when they finally did realize it, that potential was, sadly, never realized. When SPIDER-MAN was finally adapted as a limited TV series, starring Nicholas Hammond in the title role, the resulting show had little of the comic book's charm, and suffered from cheap production and a dearth of imagination.

THE SPIRIT
newspaper strip

THE SPIRIT (ABC, 1987)—TV movie; 120 minutes; color.

Credits: Executive Producers: Frank von Zerneck, Stu Samuels; Producer: Paul Aratow; Supervising Producer: Steven E. de Souza; Co-Producer: William Beaudine, Jr.; Director: Michael Schultz; Screenplay: Steven E. de Souza; Camera: Frank Thackery; Music: Barry Goldenberg.

Cast: Sam Jones; Nana Visitor; Bumper Robinson; Garry Walberg; Les Lannom; McKinlay Robinson; Daniel Davis; Philip Baker Hall; John Allen; Sarah Dammann; Janens Rotblatt; Ernestine Mercer; Annabal Liende; Joe Newnow; Robert Patorelli; Bill Marcus; Edmund Cambridge; Bobby Jacoby.

Created by Will Eisner as a seven-page color Sunday newspaper supplement and distributed by the Register and Tribune Syndicate, this unique strip premiered in June of 1940 and ran until September of 1952 (sporadic revival attempts were made in the '50s, '60s, and '70s). Few cartoonists have been able to match Eisner's imagination and visual flair; his cinematic artwork and delightful tongue-in-cheek scripting have made THE SPIRIT a high-water mark in its field. Eisner's Denny Colt is a former detective who, wearing a mask to conceal his identity, lives beneath a cemetery and occasionally ventures forth to oppose the criminal element.

An announced film version, which was to have been scripted by Harlan Ellison and directed by William Friedkin, never materialized, and when Eisner's bizarre character finally was adapted to film, it was in a lackluster made-for-TV movie.

SPY SMASHER
comic book
Fawcett Publications

SPY SMASHER (Republic, 1942)—theatrical serial; 12 chapters, first chapter approximately 30 minutes, remaining chapters approximately 20 minutes each.

SPY SMASHER (Republic, 1942): Marguerite Chapman, Kane Richmond.

Credits: Associate Producer: William J. O'Sullivan; Director: William Witney; Screenplay: Ronald Davidson, Norman S. Hall, Joseph Poland, William Lively, Joseph O'Donnell; Camera: Reggie Lanning; Music: Mort Glickman; Special Effects: Howard Lydecker.

Cast: Kane Richmond (Spy Smasher); Sam Flint (Admiral Corby); Marguerite Chapman (Eve Corby); Hans Schumm (The Mask); Tristram Coffin (Drake); Frank Corsaro (Durand); Hans Von Morhart (Captain Gerhardt); Georges Renavent (The Governor); Robert O. Davis (Colonel Von Kohr); Henry Zynda (Lazar); Paul Bryar (Lawler); Tom London (Crane); Richard Bond (Hayes); Crane Whitley (Dr. Hauser); John James (Steve).

Chapter Titles: (1) America Beware; (2) Human Target; (3) The Iron Coffin; (4) Stratosphere Invaders; (5) Descending Doom; (6) The Invisible Witness; (7) The Secret Weapon; (8) Sea Raiders; (9) Highway Racketeers; (10) 2700° Fahrenheit; (11) A Heroe's Death; (12) V. . . -.

Note: A 100-minute feature version, SPY SMASHER RETURNS, was re-edited from the original footage in 1966.

Created by writer Bill Parker and artists C. C. Beck and Pete Costanza, SPY SMASHER premiered in WHIZ COMICS #1 in February of 1940. Like Captain America, Spy Smasher was a dedicated and unstoppable costumed foe of the World War II Axis powers, and, also like Captain America, Spy Smasher was very much a creation of and for his time—he could not exist for long outside of the World War II milieu, and once the war ended, so did the character's appeal. Attempts to maintain the strip by rechristening the postwar character Crime Smasher were unsuccessful, and the ailing strip finally expired with WHIZ COMICS #63 in March of 1953.

The Republic serial adaptation of the strip is one of the finest serials ever made, and arguably that studio's best cliffhanger effort, featuring excellent performances by Kane Richmond and Marguerite Chapman, excellent photography and miniature work, and a rousing musical score that incorporates Beethoven's Fifth Symphony to good effect.

STEVE CANYON
newspaper strip

STEVE CANYON (NBC, 1958–59)—TV series; each episode 30 minutes.

Credits: Producers: David Haft, Michael Meshekoff; Music: Walter Schumann, Nathan Scott.

Cast: Dean Fredericks (Lt. Col. Steve Canyon); Jerry Paris (Maj. Willie Williston); Abel Fernandez (Police Chief Hagedorn).

Created by Milton Caniff for the Field Newspaper Syndicate, this famous aviation-adventure strip premiered in January of 1947.

SUPERBOY
comic book
National Periodicals/DC Comics

SUPERBOY (1961)—TV pilot; 30 minutes.

Credits: Producer: Whitney Ellsworth; Director: George Blair; Screenplay: Vernon E. Clark, Whitney Ellsworth; Camera: Dick Rawlins; Art Director: Jack Collins; Editor: John B. Woelz;

Production Supervisor: Joe Wonder; Audio Supervisor: Al Lincoln; Sound Editor: Chuck Overhulser; Music Editor: Milton Lustig; Set Decorator: Charles Thompson; Wardrobe: Walt Hoffman; Makeup: Fred B. Phillips; Casting: Harvey Clermont.

Cast: Johnny Rockwell (Superboy/Clark Kent); Bunny Henning (Lana Lang); Ross Elliott (Fred Drake); Monty Margetts (Martha Kent); Charles Maxwell (Gunner Ferde); Robert Williams (Police Chief Parker); Richard Reeves (Shifty Barnes); Yvonne White (Miss Gibson); Stacy Harris (Jake Ferde); Jimmy Bates (Jimmie Dean); Ray Walker (Mr. Edlund); Trudy Ellison (Donna Givney).

SUPERBOY (Syndicated, 1989)—TV series; each episode 30 minutes; color.

Credits: Executive Producer: Ilya Salkind; Producer: Bob Simmonds; Music: Kevin Kiner; Special Effects: Orson Ochoa.

Cast: John Haymes Newton (Superboy/Clark Kent); Stacy Haiduk (Lana Lang); James Calvert (T. J. White); Duriel Harris; Doug Barr; Noah Meeks; Fred Broderson; Jay Glick; Paul J. Darby.

See SUPERMAN for details.

SUPERGIRL
comic book
National Periodicals/DC Comics

SUPERGIRL (Tri-Star, 1984)—theatrical feature; 114 minutes; color.

Credits: Executive Producer: Ilya Salkind; Producer: Timothy Burrill; Director: Jeannot Szwarc; Screenplay; David Odell; Camera: Alan Hume; Editor: Malcolm Cooke; Production Design: Richard MacDonald; Art Director: Terry Ackland-Snow; Music: Jerry Goldsmith; Costumes: Emma Porteus; Sound: Derek Ball, Robin Gregory; Special Effects: Derek Meddings; Optical Special Effects: Roy Field; Travelling Matte Consultant: Dennis Bartlett; Set Decorator: Peter Young; Special Effects Supervisor: John Evans; Flying Effects: Bob Harman; Miniatures: Terry Reed, Roy Scott, Robert Scott, Tadeusz Krzanowski, Rodger Shaw; Stunts: Alf Joint; Process Camera: Ronald Goodman; Visual Effects Camera: Paul Wilson; Video Coordinator: Charles Warren; Matte Artists: Doug Ferris, Charles Stoneman.

Cast: Faye Dunaway (Selena); Helen Slater (Supergirl/Linda Lee); Peter O'Toole (Zaltar); Peter Cooke (Nigel); Brenda Vaccaro (Bianca); Mia Farrow (Alura); Simon Ward (Zor-El); Marc McClure (Jimmy Olsen); Hart Bochner (Ethan); Maureen Teely (Lucy Lane); David Healy (Mr. Danvers); Sandra Dickinson (Pretty Young Lady); Robyn Mandell (Myra); Jennifer Landor (Muffy); Diana Ricardo (Mrs. Murray); Nancy Lippold (Billy Jo); Sonya Leite (Betsy); Virginia Greig (Jodie); Nancy Wood (Nancy).

Created by comic-book editor Mort Weisinger and writer Otto Binder in an apparent effort to wring every last dime of potential cash from the Superman mythos, Supergirl, a hitherto unknown relation of Superman's and a belated arrival from the destroyed planet Krypton, made her debut in ACTION COMICS #252 in May of 1959. The initial artist was Al Plastino, then Jim Mooney eventually became the strip's permanent illustrator.

The feature-film adaptation offered a surprisingly sincere performance from Helen Slater in the title role, but very little else of merit, and suffered from the same poor technical work that plagued the Christopher Reeve SUPERMAN films.

SUPERMAN
comic book
National Periodicals/DC Comics

SUPERMAN (Columbia, 1948)—theatrical serial; 15 chapters, first chapter approximately 30 minutes, remaining chapters approximately 20 minutes each.

Credits: Producer: Sam Katzman; Directors: Spencer G. Bennet, Thomas Carr; Screenplay: Arthur Hoerl, Lewis Clay, Royal Cole; Camera: Ira H. Morgan; Music: Mischa Bakaleinikoff; Editor: Earl Turner; Assistant Director: R. M. Andrews; Second Unit Director: Thomas Carr.

Cast: Kirk Alyn (Superman/Clark Kent); Noel Neill (Lois Lane); Lyle Talbot (Luthor); Tommy Bond (Jimmy Olsen); Carol Forman (Spider Lady); George Meeker (Driller); Jack Ingram (Anton); Pierre Watkin (Perry White); Terry Frost (Brock); Charles King (Conrad); Charles Quigley (Dr. Hackett); Herbert Rawlinson (Dr. Graham); Forrest Taylor (Leeds); Stephen Carr (Morgan); Rusty Wescoatt (Elton).

Chapter Titles: (1) Superman Comes to Earth; (2) Depths of the Earth; (3) The Reducer Ray; (4) Man of Steel; (5) A Job for Superman; (6) Superman in Danger; (7) Into the Electric Furnace; (8) Superman to the Rescue; (9) Irresistible Force; (10) Between Two Fires; (11) Superman's Dilemma; (12) Blast in the Depths; (13) Hurled to Destruction; (14) Superman at Bay; (15) The Payoff.

Note: The original release prints of this serial were tinted sepia.

ATOM MAN VS. SUPERMAN (Columbia, 1950)—theatrical serial; 15 chapters, first chapter approximately 30 minutes, remaining chapters approximately 20 minutes each.

SUPERMAN (Columbia, 1948): Kirk Alyn as the title hero.

SUPERMAN (Columbia, 1948): Noel Neill, Tommy Bond, George Meeker, Kirk Alyn, and Carol Forman.

ATOM MAN VS. SUPERMAN (Columbia, 1950): Noel Neill watches as Kirk Alyn apprehends the villainous Lyle Talbot (as Lex Luthor).

Credits: Producer: Sam Katzman; Director: Spencer G. Bennet; Screenplay: George H. Plympton, Joseph F. Poland, David Mathews; Camera: Ira H. Morgan; Music: Mischa Bakaleinikoff; Editor: Earl Turner; Assistant Director: R. M. Andrews; Second Unit Director: Derwin Abrahams.

Cast: Kirk Alyn (Superman/Clark Kent); Noel Neill (Lois Lane); Lyle Talbot (Luthor); Tommy Bond (Jimmy Olsen); Pierre Watkin (Perry White); Jack Ingram (Foster); Don Harvey (Alber); Rusty Wescoatt (Carl); Terry Frost (Baer); Wally West (Dorr); Paul Stader (Lawson); George Robotham (Earl).

Chapter Titles: (1) Superman Flies Again; (2) Atom Man Appears; (3) Ablaze in the Sky; (4) Superman Meets Atom Man; (5) Atom Man Tricks Superman; (6) Atom Man's Challenge; (7) At the Mercy of Atom Man; (8) Into the Empty Room; (9) Superman Crashes Through; (10) Atom Man's Heat Ray; (11) Luthor's Strategy; (12) Atom Man Strikes; (13) Atom Man's Flying Saucer; (14) Rocket of Vengeance; (15) Superman Saves the Universe.

SUPERMAN AND THE MOLE MEN (Lippert, 1951)— theatrical feature; 57 minutes (*GB: SUPERMAN AND THE STRANGE PEOPLE*).

Credits: Producers: Robert Maxwell, Barney A. Sarecky; Director: Lee Sholem; Screenplay: Richard Fielding (Robert Maxwell); Camera: Clark Ramsey; Editor: Al Joseph; Special Effects: Ray Mercer.

Cast: George Reeves (Superman/Clark Kent); Phyllis Coates (Lois Lane); Jeff Corey (Luke Benson); Walter Reed (Bill Corrigan); J. Farrell MacDonald (Pop Shannon); Stanley Andrews (Sheriff); Ray Walker (John Craig); Hal K. Dawson (Weber); Frank Reicher (Hospital Superintendant); Beverly

ATOM MAN VS. SUPERMAN (Columbia, 1950): Kirk Alyn in flight.

Washburn (Little Girl); Stephen Carr (Eddie); Paul Berns (Doc Saunders); Margia Dean (Mrs. Benson); Bryon Foulger (Jeff Regan); Irene Martin (Esther Pomfrey); John Phillips (Matt); Phil Warren (Deputy); John Baer (Intern); Adrienne Marden (Nurse); Billy Curtis, Jack Banbury, Jerry Marvin, Tony Baris (Mole Men).

Note: This feature was re-edited into a two-part episode of THE ADVENTURES OF SUPERMAN television series and retitled UNKNOWN PEOPLE.

THE ADVENTURES OF SUPERMAN (Syndicated, 1953–57)—TV series; 104 episodes, 30 minutes each; b/w and color.

Credits: Producers: Robert Maxwell, Bernard Luber, Whitney Ellsworth; Series Directors: Thomas Carr, Lee Sholem, Harry

SUPERMAN AND THE MOLE MEN (Lippert, 1951): Reeves demonstrates his strength to villain Jeff Corey.

SUPERMAN AND THE MOLE MEN (Lippert, 1951): George Reeves, *center*, protects Phyllis Coates from villain Jeff Corey.

Gerstad, Lew Landers, Bob Barnes, Philip Ford, Howard Bretherton, George Reeves; Series Writers: Robert Maxwell, Whitney Ellsworth, Eugene Solow, Dennis Cooper, Lee Backman, William Joyce, Ben Freeman, Doris Gilbert, Monroe Manning, Peter Dixon, Dick Hamilton, Howard Green, David Chantler, Dwight Babcock, Robert Bellem, Oliver Drake, Wilton Schiller, Ben Crocker; Camera: Harold Wellman, Harold Stine, Joseph Brice.

Cast: George Reeves (Superman/Clark Kent); Phyllis Coates, Noel Neill (Lois Lane); Jack Larson (Jimmy Olsen); John Hamilton (Perry White); Robert Shayne (Inspector Henderson); Phillips Tead (Professor Pepperwinkle); Herb Vigran (Sy Horton); Yvonne White (Ethel); Robert Rockwell (Jor-El); Aline Towne (Lara); Tom Fadden (Eben Kent); Dina Nolan (Martha Kent); Stuart Randall (Young Clark Kent).

SUPERMAN COMPILATION MOVIES—theatrical features.

These ersatz features each contained three episodes of the George Reeves TV series. The episodes were not re-edited, and were simply run back-to-back with complete TV opening and closing credits. All were released by Twentieth Century-Fox in 1954. The titles are: SUPERMAN AND SCOTLAND YARD; SUPERMAN AND THE JUNGLE DEVIL; SUPERMAN FLIES AGAIN; SUPERMAN IN EXILE; and SUPERMAN'S PERIL.

SUPERPUP (1958)—TV pilot; 30 minutes

Credits: Producer: Whitney Ellsworth; Director: Cal Howard; Screenplay: Cal Howard, Whitney Ellsworth; Camera: Joseph Biroc; Editor: Sam Waxman; Art Director: Lou Croxton; Set Decorator: Glenn Thompson; Special Effects: Thol Simonson; Photographic Effects: Jack Rabin, Louis DeWitt; Sound: Ryder

Sound Services; Assistant Director: Edward Haldeman; Production Manager and Assistant Director: Ben Chapman.

Cast: Billy Curtis (Superpup/Bark Bent); Ruth Delfino (Pamela Poodle); Angelo Rossito (Perry Bite); Frank Delfino (Sergeant Beagle); Harry Monty (Professor Sheepdip); Sadie Defino (Sheepdip's Dupe).

Note: This was a juvenile satire of SUPERMAN, filmed by the producers of the George Reeves TV series.

SUPERMAN (Warner Bros., 1973)—non-theatrical feature; 104 minutes; color.

This compilation feature contained four episodes of the TV series.

IT'S A BIRD, IT'S A PLANE, IT'S SUPERMAN (ABC, 1975)—TV special; 120 minutes; color.

Credits: Producer: Norman Twain; Associate Producer: Elliot Alexander; Director: Jack Regas; Screenplay: Romeo Muller; Music: Fred Werner; Musical Book: David Newman, Robert Benton; Original Music: Charles Strouse, Lee Adams; Art Director: Ken Johnson; Choreography: Alex Plasschsert.

Cast: David Wilson (Superman/Clark Kent); Lesley Ann Warren (Lois Lane); Allen Ludden (Perry White); David Wayne (Dr. Sedgwick); Ken Mars (Max Mencken); Loretta Swit (Sydney Carlton); Gary Owens (Narrator).

Note: This low-budget special was adapted from the Broadway musical.

SUPERMAN (Warner Bros., 1978)—theatrical feature; 143 minutes; color.

SUPERMAN AND THE MOLE MEN (Lippert, 1951): A publicity portrait of George Reeves.

Credits: Producer: Pierre Spengler; Director: Richard Donner; Screenplay: Mario Puzo, David Newman, Leslie Newman, Robert Benton (Original Story: Mario Puzo); Camera: Geoffrey Unsworth; Music: John Williams; Editor: Stuart Baird; Production Design: John Barry; Costumes: Yvonne Blake; Special Effects: Colin Chivers, Roy Field, Derek Meddings, Zoran Perisic, Denys Coop, Leslie Bowie; Music and Lyrics (for the song "Can You Read My Mind?"): John Williams, Leslie Bricusse; Vocal: Margot Kidder; Makeup: Philip Rhodes, Basil Newall, Kay Freeborn, Graham Freeborn, Nick Maley, Sylvia Croft, Connie Reeve, Louis Lane, Jamie Brown.

Cast: Marlon Brando (Jor-El); Gene Hackman (Lex Luthor); Christopher Reeve (Superman/Clark Kent); Ned Beatty (Otis);

Jackie Cooper (Perry White); Glenn Ford (Pa Kent); Trevor Howard (First Elder); Margot Kidder (Lois Lane); Jack O'Halloran (Non); Valerie Perrine (Eve Teschmacher); Maria Schell (Vond-Ah); Terence Stamp (General Zod); Phyllis Thaxter (Ma Kent); Susannah York (Lara); Jeff East (Young Clark Kent); Marc McClure (Jimmy Olsen); Sarah Douglas (Ursa); Harry Andrews (Second Elder); Lee Quigley (Baby Kal-El); Aaron Smolinski (Baby Clark Kent); Diane Sherry (Lana Lang); Jeff Atcheson (Coach); Jill Ingham (Perry White's Seccretary); Rex Reed (Himself); Weston Gavin (Mugger); George Harris II (Patrolman Mooney); Rex Everhardt (Desk Sergeant); Jayne Tottman (Little Girl); Larry Hagman (Major); Paul Tuerpe (Sergeant Hayley); Phil Brown; Bill Bailey (State Senators); Chief Tug Smith (Indian Chief); Roy Stevens (Warden); Kirk Alyn, Noel Neill (Couple on Train); Bob Dahdah (Newspaper Customer); Vass Anderson; John Hallis; James Garbutt; Michael Gover; David Neal; William Russell; Penelope Lee; John Stuart; Alan Cullen; Larry Lamb; James Brackington; John Cassady; John F. Parker; Antony Scott; Ray Evans; Su Shifrin; Miguel Brown; Vincent Marzello; Benjamin Feitelson; Lise Hilboldt; Leueen Willoughby; Pieter Stuyck; Stephen Kahan; Ray Hassett; Randy Jurgenson; Malf Russo; Colin Skeaping; Bo Rucker; Paul Avery; David Maxt; Michael Harrigan; John Cording; Raymond Thompson; Oz Clarke; Frank Lazarus; Brian Protheroe; Lawrence Trimble; Robert Whelan; David Calder; Norwick Duff; Keith Alexander; Michael Ensign; Graham McPherson; David Yorston; Robert O'Neill; Robert MacLeod; John Ratzenberger; Alan Tilvern; Burnell Tucker; Norman Warwick; Chuck Julian; Colin Etherington; Mark Wynter.

SUPERMAN II (Warner Bros., 1980)—theatrical feature; 127 minutes; color.

Credits: Producer: Pierre Spengler; Director: Richard Lester; Screenplay: Mario Puzo, David Newman, Leslie Newman

THE ADVENTURES OF SUPERMAN (1953): George Reeves soars through the
night sky in this scene from the TV series.

(Original Story: Mario Puzo); Camera: Geoffrey Unsworth,
Robert Paynter; Music: Ken Thorne (Original Themes: John
Williams); Editor: John Victor-Smith; Production Design: John
Barry, Peter Murton; Art Director: Maurice Fowler; Costumes:
Yvonne Blake, Susan Yelland; Special Effects: Colin Chivers,
Roy Field, Zoran Perisic; Makeup: Stuart Freeborn.

Cast: Gene Hackman (Lex Luthor); Christopher Reeve
(Superman/Clark Kent); Ned Beatty (Otis); Jackie Cooper
(Perry White); Sarah Douglas (Ursa); Margot Kidder (Lois
Lane); Jack O'Halloran (Non); Valerie Perrine (Eve Teschma-
cher); Susannah York (Lara); Clifton James (Sheriff); E. G.
Marshall (The President); Marc McClure (Jimmy Olsen);
Terence Stamp (General Zod); Leueen Willoughby (Leueen);
Robin Pappas (Alice); Roger Kemp (Spokesman); Roger

Brierley, Anthony Milner, Richard Griffiths (Terrorists); Melissa Wiltsie (Nun); Alain DeHay (Gendarme); Marc Boyle (C.R.S. Man); Alan Stuart (Cab Driver); John Ratzenberger, Shane Rimmer (Controllers); John Morton (Nate); Jim Dowdell (Boris); Angus McInnes (Warden); Antony Sher (Bellboy); Elva May Hoover (Mother); Hadley Kay (Jason); Todd Woodcroft (Father); John Hollis (Krypton Elder); Gordon Rollings (Fisherman); Peter Whitman (Deputy); Bill Bailey (J. J.); Dinny Powell (Boog); Hal Galili (Man at Bar); Marcus D'Amico (Willie); Jackie Cooper (Dino); Richard Parmentier (Reporter); Don Fellows (General); Michael J. Shannon (President's Aide); Tony Sibbald (Presidential Imposter); Tommy Duggan (Diner Owner); Pamela Mandell (Waitress); Pepper Martin (Rocky); Eugene Lipinsky (News Vendor); Cleon Spencer, Carl Parris (Kids).

SUPERMAN III (Warner Bros., 1983)—theatrical feature; 123 minutes; color.

Credits: Producer: Pierre Spengler; Director: Richard Lester; Screenplay: David Newman, Leslie Newman; Camera: Robert Paynter; Music: Ken Thorne, John Williams; Editor: John Victor-Smith; Production Design: Peter Murton; Art Director: Brian Ackland-Snow, Charles Bishop, Terry Ackland-Snow; Costumes: Vangie Harrison; Special Effects: Roy Field, Colin Chivers, Martin Gutteridge, Brian Warner; Song Lyrics: Giorgio Moroder; Makeup: Stuart Freeborn.

Cast: Christopher Reeve (Superman/Clark Kent); Richard Pryor (Gus Gorman); Jackie Cooper (Perry White); Margot Kidder (Lois Lane); Annette O'Toole (Lana Lang); Annie Ross (Vera Webster); Pamela Stephenson (Lorelei Ambrosia); Robert Vaughn (Ross Webster); Marc McClure (Jimmy Olsen); Nancy Roberts (Unemployment Clerk); Graham Stark (Blind Man); Henry Wolf (Penguin Man); Gordon Rollings (Man in Cap); Peter Wear (Bank Robber); Justin Case (Mime); Bob Todd

(Dignified Gent); Terry Camilleri (Delivery Man); Stefan Kalipha (Data School Instructor); Helen Horton (Miss Henderson); Lou Hirsch (Fred); Bill Reimbold (Wages Man); Shane Rimmer (State Policeman); Al Matthews (Fire Chief); Barry Dennen (Dr. McClean); Enid Saunders (Minnie Bannister); Kevin Harrison Cork (D. J.); Robert G. Henderson (Mr. Simpson); Paul Kaether (Ricky); R. J. Bell (Mr. Stokis); Pamela Mandell (Mrs. Stokis); Peter Whitman (Man at Cash Point); Ronnie Brody (Husband); Sandra Dickinson (Wife); Philip Gilbert (Newsreader); Pat Starr (Scientist); Gordon Signer (Mayor); John Bluthal (Pisa Vendor); George Chisholm (Street Sweeper); David Fielder (Olympic Runner); Robert Beatty (Tanker Captain); Chris Malcolm, Larry Lamb (Miners); Gavin O'Herlihy.

SUPERMAN IV: THE QUEST FOR PEACE (Cannon/ Warner Bros., 1987)—theatrical feature; 88 minutes; color.

Credits: Producers: Menaheim Golan, Yoram Globas; Director: Sidney J. Furie; Screenplay: Lawrence Konner, Mark Rosenthal (Original Story: Lawrence Konner, Mark Rosenthal, Christopher Reeve); Camera: Ernest Day; Music: John Williams, Alexander Courage; Editor: John Shirley; Production Design: John Graysmark; Music Director: Alexander Courage; Art Director: Leslie Tomkins; Set Design: Peter Young; Costumes: John Bloomfield; Special Effects: John Evans, Richard Conway, Harrison Ellenshaw.

Cast: Christopher Reeve (Superman/Clark Kent); Gene Hackman (Lex Luthor); Jackie Cooper (Perry White); Marc McClure (Jimmy Olsen); Jon Cryer (Lenny); Sam Wanamaker (David Warfield); Mark Pillow (Nuclear Man); Mariel Hemingway (Lacy Warfield); Margot Kidder (Lois Lane).

SUPERMAN'S 50TH ANNIVERSARY (CBS, 1988)—TV special; 60 minutes; color.

This TV special featured clips from the various SUPER-MAN movies and TV shows.

Created by writer Jerry Siegel and artist Joe Shuster, superman—the greatest of all comic strip heroes—premiered in ACTION COMICS #1 in June of 1938. The strip was such a wildfire success that Superman was quickly awarded his own book. Eventually, an entire line of spin-off books appeared, featuring virtually every friend and acquaintance of Superman's, and even his own adolescence was scrutinized in SUPERBOY comics (q.v.).

Although a series of excellent Technicolor cartoons, animated by the Max Fleischer studios, appeared in the early 1940s, it was not until 1948 that SUPERMAN was finally adapted to the screen in live-action form, in a serial produced by Columbia Pictures. There had been an earlier attempt, by Republic Pictures, to adapt the character, but when Republic balked at the restrictive licensing requirements made by National Periodical Publications (later DC Comics), the publishers of SUPERMAN, they cancelled the project and hastily retooled the script, eliminating the SUPERMAN characters and ultimately filming it as THE MYSTERIOUS DR. SATAN (1940), which was, incredibly, one of Republic's better cliffhangers, despite the patchwork screenplay. In the 1948 Columbia Pictures serial SUPERMAN, Kirk Alyn starred in the title role. Although the film was cheap, with cut-rate cartoon animation used for the flying scenes and other special effects and was hampered by some inept acting in the supporting roles (particularly the very beautiful but untalented Carol Forman as the villainous Spider Lady), Alyn himself was the perfect flesh-and-blood embodiment of Superman, and the picture was extremely popular. Like Universal's FLASH GORDON, SUPERMAN was such a success that it played evening performances at first-run theaters, and it was the most profitable serial produced by Columbia Pictures. Noel Neill was Lois Lane, exhibiting a cuteness and vitality that she lacked when she resumed the role in the much-later TV series starring

George Reeves, and Tommy Bond played a surprisingly aggressive Jimmy Olsen, with Pierre Watkin lending sarcastic support as *Daily Planet* newspaper editor Perry White.

The inevitable sequel, ATOM MAN VS. SUPERMAN, was comprised of similar elements, although better support (and better acting) was provided by Lyle Talbot as Superman's comic-book nemesis Lex Luthor. As in the first serial, ATOM MAN VS. SUPERMAN was compromised to a degree by tacky production values and the insertion of cartoon animation for the flying scenes, but the sequel had a better plot than the original, and somewhat better pacing, resulting in another success for Columbia. For years afterwards, promotional trailers for Columbia serials would exploit the fame of the studio's two SUPERMAN cliffhangers, evidently in the forlorn hope that a little of their success could be repeated, with the trailers for such Sam Katzman–produced turkeys as CONGO BILL fervently bleating ". . . from the company that gave you SUPERMAN!" at the slightest opportunity.

Barely a year after ATOM MAN VS. SUPERMAN, a new screen Superman appeared in the person of George Reeves, who essayed the role in a low-budget feature, SUPERMAN AND THE MOLE MEN. A bizarre mixture of THE OX-BOW INCIDENT and THE DAY THE EARTH STOOD STILL, SUPERMAN AND THE MOLE MEN, despite flaccid pacing and a hackneyed musical score (the editing and music were improved considerably when the feature was re-edited and re-scored as a two-part episode of the later Reeves TV series), is one of the more intriguing 1950s fantasy films, and certainly one of the best movies released by Lippert Pictures. Reeves, who did not resemble his comic-book counterpoint as closely as Alyn had, nevertheless had more of a physical *presence* than Alyn, and was a far better actor. Actress Phyllis Coates, who played girl reporter Lois Lane in the film and the first season of the later series, told this writer of Reeves:

> He was a dear to work with, a very professional, slick guy.
> He'd done a lot of very prestigious work before the

SUPERMAN shows. By then, we both felt we'd hit the bottom of the barrel. When we finally met, we had a drink and toasted each other. He said, "Well, babe, this is the bottom of the barrel!" and I said, "Yep!" But we both needed the work and there was a nice chemistry there. . . . We shot very fast—we averaged twenty-four pages of dialogue a day. . . . George had a photographic mind. I did not, although I had a very good memory. George would just read the script a couple of times and he had it. It pulled me up just to work with him.

Reeves and Coates promptly went on to continue their roles in the long-running syndicated TV series THE ADVENTURES OF SUPERMAN. The first season of twenty-six episodes was somewhat similar in mood and tone to SUPERMAN AND THE MOLE MEN: dark, somber, and faintly menacing, a surprisingly adult film-noir ambience that would frequently include death and murder in the sometimes violent plots. More of a cop show with Superman occasionally intruding as a fantasy element, the photography and special effects, particularly many of the flying scenes, were generally excellent, and the first twenty-six episodes remain the most compelling in the series. With the beginning of the second season, the tone of the series shifted somewhat; Coates had left to be replaced by Kirk Alyn's Lois, Noel Neill, and there were other differences as well, with the entire approach of the series becoming lighter, and, as the show progressed, even more openly comedic, with a lot of slapstick byplay from Jack Larson as cub reporter Jimmy Olsen. From the third season on, the show was filmed in color (although it was not distributed in this format until 1965), and the budget, always tight, was by this point insufficient; the same few stock shots of Reeves in flight were incessantly repeated, and the action was almost invariably restricted to a couple of threadbare sets per episode. Reeves, too, was growing tired and lackluster in his performance, not to mention increasingly hefty and physically unfit for the role. Reeves continued on, though, until his untimely death (under mysterious circumstances) at the age of forty-five in 1959. He even directed a couple of the last episodes. Even at its worst, THE ADVENTURES OF SUPERMAN was always entertaining, largely because of Reeves himself and his professionalism and genuine warmth in the role. For a generation of Americans, George Reeves remains the only true Superman, and was the only actor to impart any sort of emotional depth to the character, despite claims to the contrary by his successor, Christopher Reeve.

The more recent Christopher Reeve features seem disappointing and unsatisfying, and despite their multimillion-dollar budgets, look amazingly cheap, with shoddy photography and special effects that are, in some instances, inferior to those in the TV series!

SWAMP THING
comic book
National Periodicals/DC Comics

SWAMP THING (Embassy, 1982)—theatrical feature; 90 minutes; color.

Credits: Producers: Benjamin Melniker, Michael E. Uslan; Director: Wes Craven; Screenplay: Wes Craven; Camera: Robin Goodwin; Music: Harry Manfredini; Editor: Richard Bracken; Production Design: Robb Wilson King; Art Directors: David Nichols King, Rhoda Neal; Costumes: Patricia Bolomet, Bennett Choate, Paul A. Simmons; Makeup: William Munns; Stunts: Ted Duncan.

Cast: Louis Jourdan (Arcane); Adrienne Barbeau (Alice Cable); Ray Wise (Dr. Alec Holland); David Hess (Ferret); Nicholas Worth (Bruno); Don Knight (Ritter); Al Ruban (Charlie); Dick Durock (Swamp Thing); Ben Bates (Arcane Monster); Nannette Brown (Dr. Linda Holland); Reggie Batts (Jude); Mimi Meyer (Secretary); Karen Price (Messenger); Bill

Erickson (Young Agent); Dov Gottsfeld (Commando); Tommy Madden (Little Bruno).

THE RETURN OF THE SWAMP THING (Miramax, 1989)— theatrical feature; 88 minutes; color.

Credits: Producers: Ben Melniker, Michael Uslan; Executive Producers: Tom Kuhn, Charles Mitchell; Director: Jim Wynorski; Screenplay: Derek Spencer, Grant Morris; Camera: Zoran Hochstatter; Editor: Leslie Rosenthal; Music: Chuck Cirino; Production Design: Robert Wilson King; Set Decorator: Frank Galline; Sound: Blake Wilcox; Special Effects: Special Effects International; Co-Producer: Annette Cirillo; Assistant Directors: Bruce Meade, Eric Moss; Casting: Shay Griffin, Joey Alfieris.

Cast: Louis Jourdan (Dr. Anton Arcane); Heather Locklear (Abby Arcane); Sarah Douglas (Dr. Lana Zurrell); Dick Durock (Swamp Thing); Ace Mask (Dr. Rochelle); Joey Sagal (Gunn).

SWAMP THING (USA Cable Network, 1990)—syndicated TV series; 30 minutes each episode.

Credits: Executive Producers: Benjamin Melniker, Michael E. Uslan; Supervising Producer: Joseph Stefano; Producer: Boris Malden; Story Editors: Sandra Berg, Judith Berg, Music: Christopher L. Stone; Production Manager: Charles Ziarko; Supervising Editor: John Elias; Swamp Thing Body Unit Design: Carl Fullerton, Neal Martz; Makeup Effects: Alterian Studios.

Cast: Dick Durock (Swamp Thing).

A horror strip drawn by Bernie Wrightson, the Swamp Thing character, a biochemist horribly disfigured and transformed in a lab explosion, first appeared in HOUSE OF SECRETS #92 in June of 1971, and the monstrous anti-hero was quickly awarded his own comic book. The two films based on the character are unremarkable, never achieving the brooding atmosphere of Wrightson's artwork.

TAILSPIN TOMMY
newspaper strip

TAILSPIN TOMMY (Universal, 1934)—theatrical serial; 12 chapters, each chapter approximately 20 minutes.

Credits: Producer: Milton Gatzert; Associate Producer: Henry MacRae; Director: Louis Friedlander; Screenplay: Norman S. Hall, Vin Moore, Basil Dickey, Ella O'Neill; Camera: Richard Fryer, William Sickner; Editors: Saul Goodkind, Edward Todd, Al Akst, Irving Applebaum.

Cast: Maurice Murphy (Tailspin Tommy); Patricia Farr (Betty Lou Barnes); Noah Beery, Jr. (Skeeter); Belle Daube (Mrs. Tompkins); Lee Beggs (Deacon Grimes); Grant Withers (Milt Howe); Walter Miller (Bruce Hoyt); Clarence A. Browne (Paul Smith); Edmund Cobb (Speed Walton); John Davidson (Tiger Taggart); Monte Montague (Cliff); Jack Leonard (Al); Bud Osborne (Gease Rowley); William Desmond (Sloane).

Chapter Titles: (1) Death Flies the Mail; (2) The Mail Goes Through; (3) Sky Bandits; (4) The Copper Room; (5) The Night Flight; (6) The Baited Trap; (7) Tommy to the Rescue; (8) The Thrill of Death; (9) The Earth God's Roar; (10) Death at the Controls; (11) Rushing Waters; (12) Littleville's Big Day.

TAILSPIN TOMMY IN THE GREAT AIR MYSTERY (Universal, 1935)—theatrical serial; 12 chapters, each chapter approximately 20 minutes.

Credits: Associate Producer: Henry MacRae; Director: Ray Taylor; Screenplay: Raymond Cannon, George Plympton, Basil Dickey, Robert Hershon, Ella O'Neill; Camera: John Hickson, Leonard Galezio, William Sickner, Richard Fryer, Editors: Saul Goodkind, Edward Todd, Alvin Todd, Al Akst; Art Director: Ralph Berger.

Cast: Clark Williams (Tommy); Jean Rogers (Betty Lou); Noah Beery, Jr. (Skeeter); Delphine Drew (Inez Casmetto); Bryant Washburn (Ned Curtis); Helen Brown (Mrs. Tompkins).

Chapter Titles: (1) Wreck of the Dirigible; (2) The Roaring Fire God; (3) Hurled from the Skies; (4) A Bolt from the Blue; (5) The Torrent; (6) Flying Death; (7) The Crash in the Clouds; (8) Wings of Disaster; (9) Crossed and Double-crossed; (10) The Dungeon of Doom; (11) Desperate Changes; (12) The Last Stand.

DANGER FLIGHT (Monogram, 1939)—theatrical feature; 61 minutes.

Credits: Producer: Paul Malvern; Director: Howard Bretherton; Screenplay: Byron Morgan, Edwin C. Parsons; Camera: Fred Jackman, Jr.; Editor: Edward Schroeder.

Cast: John Trent (Tailspin Tommy); Marjorie Reynolds (Betty Lou); Milburn Stone (Skeeter); Jason Robards, Sr. (Smith); Tommy Baker (Whitey); Dennis Moore (Duke); Julius Tannen (Dawson); Edwin Parker (Williams); Joe Bernard (Brown); Harry Harvey, Jr. (Johnny); Walter Wills (Cap).

MYSTERY PLANE (Monogram, 1939)—theatrical feature; 60 minutes (*a.k.a.* SKY PILOT).

Credits: Producer: Paul Malvern; Director: George Waggner; Screenplay: Paul Shefield, Joseph West, George Waggner (Original Story: Hal Forrest); Camera: Archie Stout; Special Effects: Fred Jackman; Music: Fred Sunucci; Editor: Carl Pierson.

Cast: John Trent (Tailspin Tommy); Milburn Stone (Skeeter); Marjorie Reynolds (Betty Lou); Jason Robards, Sr. (Paul); Peter George Lynn (Brandy); Lucien Littlefield (Winslow); Polly Ann Young (Anita); Sayre Deering (Fred); Tommy Bupp (Tommy as a Child); Bettsy Gay (Betty Lou as a Child).

SKY PATROL (Monogram, 1939)—theatrical feature; 61 minutes.

Credits: Producer: Paul Malvern; Director: Howard Bretherton; Screenplay: Joseph West, George Waggner, Norman S. Parker; Camera: Fred Jackman, Jr.; Editor: Carl Pierson.

Cast: John Trent (Tailspin Tommy); Marjorie Reynolds (Betty Lou); Milburn Stone (Skeeter); Jackie Coogan (Carter); Jason Robards, Sr. (Smith); Bryant Washburn (Bainbridge); Boyd Irwin (Colonel); Leroy Mason (Mitch); John Peters (Jackson); Johnny Day (Ryan); Dickie James (Bobby).

STUNT PILOT (Monogram, 1939)—theatrical feature; 62 minutes.

Credits: Producer: Paul Malvern; Director: George Waggner; Screenplay: Joseph West, George Waggner, W. Scott Darling (Original Story: Hal Forrest); Camera: Fred B. Jackman, Jr.; Music: Fleming Allan, Carl Winge; Editor: Carl Pierson.

Cast: John Trent (Tailspin Tommy); Marjorie Reynolds (Betty Lou); Milburn Stone (Skeeter); Jason Robards, Sr. (Smith); George Meeker (Martin); Pat O'Malley (Sheehan); Wesley Barry (Glen); George Cleveland (Sheriff); Mary Field (Ethel); Todd Sterling (Charlie); Buddy Cox (Bobby); Johnny Day (Tex); Charles Morton.

Created by writer Glen Chaffin and artist Hal Foster, TAILSPIN TOMMY ran in newspapers from 1928 to 1942, and was distributed by the Bell Syndicate. Universal Pictures based two serials on this aviation-adventure strip, and seen today these chapterplays retain a great deal of small-town period charm. The later Monogram features based on the strip were inferior to the serials, and were quickly forgotten.

TEENAGE MUTANT NINJA TURTLES
comic book

TEENAGE MUTANT NINJA TURTLES (New Line Cinema, 1990)—theatrical feature; 93 minutes.

Credits: Producers: Kim Dawson, Simon Fields, David Chan; Executive Producer: Raymond Chow; Associate Producers: Graham Cottle, Gary Propper; Director: Steve Barron; Screenplay: Todd W. Langen, Bobby Herbeck (Original Story: Bobby Herbeck); Photography (Technicolor): John Fenner; Music: John Du Prez; Sound: Lee Orloff, Steve Maslow, Michael Herbick, Gregg Landaker; Production Design: Roy Forge Smith; Art Direction: Gary Wissner; Set Design: Jerry Hall; Set Decoration: Brendan Smith, Barbara Kahn; Costume Design: John M. Hay; Stunts: Pat Johnson; Special Effects Supervisor: Joey Di Gaetano; Creature Design: Jim Henson's Creature Shop; Creature Designers: Peter Brooke, Nigel Booth, John Blakeley; Puppeteers: David Greenaway, Mark Wilson, David

Rudman, Martin P. Robinson, Kevin Clash, Ricky Boyd, Robert Tygner; Voice Casting: Barbara Harris.

Cast: Judith Hoag (April O'Neil); Elias Koteas (Casey Jones); Joch Pais (Raphael); Michelan Sisti (Michelangelo); Leif Tilden (Donatello); David Forman (Leonardo); Michael Turney (Danny Pennington); Jay Patterson (Charles Pennington); Raymond Gerra (Chief Sterns); James Saito (The Shredder); Toshishiro Obata (Tatsu); Robbie Rist, Kevin Clash, Brian Tochi, David McCharen, Michael McConnohie, Corey Feldman (Voices).

The Teenage Mutant Ninja Turtles (ordinary turtles mutated into anthropomorphic form) first appeared as an underground comic book, created by Kevin Eastman and Peter Laird. A cheaply animated television cartoon adaptation achieved a surprising degree of popularity, the subsequent and inevitable juvenile-oriented merchandising boom eventually leading to the production of a live-action feature film. Although the spoofy, tongue-in-cheek turtle characters looked rubbery and unconvincing on-screen, the film was good-natured enough (with director Steve Barron wisely refusing to take the crass material seriously), and generally inoffensive.

TERRY AND THE PIRATES
newspaper strip

TERRY AND THE PIRATES (Columbia, 1940)—theatrical serial; 15 chapters, first chapter approximately 30 minutes, remaining chapters approximately 20 minutes each.

Credits: Producer: Larry Darmour; Director: James W. Horne; Screenplay: Mark Layton, George Morgan, Joseph Levering;

TERRY AND THE PIRATES (Columbia, 1940): Granville Owen rescues William Tracy.

Camera: James S. Brown, Jr.; Music: Lee Zahler; Editors: Dwight Caldwell, Earl Turner.

Cast: William Tracy (Terry Lee); Granville Owen (Pat Ryan); Joyce Bryant (Normandie Drake); Allen Jung (Connie); Victor De Camp (Big Stoop); Sheila Darcy (Dragon Lady); Dick Curtis (Fang); J. Paul Jones (Dr. Lee); Forrest Taylor (Drake); Jack Ingram (Stanton).

Chapter Titles: (1) Into the Great Unknown; (2) The Fang Strikes; (3) The Mountain of Death; (4) The Dragon Queen Threatens; (5) At the Mercy of a Mob; (6) The Scroll of Wealth; (7) Angry Waters; (8) The Tomb of Peril: (9) Jungle Hurricane; (10) Too Many Enemies; (11) Walls of Doom; (12) No Escape;

(13) The Fatal Mistake; (14) Pyre of Death; (15) The Secret of the Temple.

TERRY AND THE PIRATES (Syndicated, 1952)—TV series; each episode 30 minutes.

Credits: Producer: Warren Lewis; Series Directors: Lew Landers, Arthur Pierson, Richard Irving; Series Writers: Oliver Crawford, Barney Sarecky, Larry Roman, Arthur Pierson, William Wolft, Norman S. Hall, Frank Burt, Irwin Shkenazy, Lou Rosoff, Gwen Bagni, John Bagni.

Cast: John Baer (Terry Lee); Gloria Saunders (The Dragon Lady); Marie Blanchard; Sandra Spence (Burma); Walter Tracy (Hot Shot Charlie); Jack Reitzen (Chopstick Joe).

Created by writer/artist Milton Caniff for the Chicago Tribune-New York News Syndicate, TERRY AND THE PI-RATES premiered in October of 1934 and ran until February of 1973. Distinguished by Caniff's unique artistic style, larger-than-life characterizations and exotic locales, the strip was immensely popular with newspaper readers, and Caniff's work retains its charm when read today. The Columbia Pictures serial adaptation, from that studio's best period, has, unfortunately, remained unavailable since its first release.

TEX GRANGER
comic book
Parents' Magazine Institute

TEX GRANGER (Columbia, 1948)—theatrical serial; 15 chapters, first chapter approximately 30 minutes, remaining chapters approximately 20 minutes each.

Credits: Producer: Sam Katzman; Director: Derwin Abrahams; Screenplay: Arthur Hoerl, Lewis Clay, Harry Fraser, Royal Cole; Camera: Ira H. Morgan; Music: Mischa Bakaleinikoff; Editor: Earl Turner; Assistant Director: Mike Eason.

Cast: Robert Kellard (Tex Granger); Peggy Stewart (Helen Kent); Buzz Henry (Tim); Duke, the Wonder Dog (Himself); Smith Ballew (Blaze Talbot); Jack Ingram (Reno); I. Stanford Jolley (Carson); Terry Frost (Adams); Jim Diehl (Conroy); Britt Wood (Sandy); Bill Brauer (Joe Hall).

Chapter Titles: (1) Tex Finds Trouble; (2) Rider of Mystery Mesa; (3) Dead or Alive; (4) Dangerous Trails; (5) Renegade Pass; (6) A Crooked Deal; (7) The Rider Unmasked; (8) Mystery of the Silver Ghost; (9) The Rider Trapped; (10) Midnight Ambush; (11) Renegade Roundup; (12) Carson's Last Draw; (13) Blaze Takes Over; (14) Riding Wild; (15) The Rider Meets Blaze.

This western-adventure strip premiered in TEX GRANGER #18 (which, prior to this issue, had been known as CALLING ALL BOYS) in June of 1948. The book was discontinued with issue #24 in September of 1949.

THUNDA
comic book
M.E. Publications

KING OF THE CONGO (Columbia, 1952)—theatrical serial; 15 chapters, first chapter approximately 30 minutes, remaining chapters approximately 20 minutes each.

Credits: Producer: Sam Katzman; Directors: Spencer G. Bennet, Wallace Grissell; Screenplay: George H. Plympton,

Royal K. Cole, Arthur Hoerl; Camera: William Whitley; Music: Mischa Bakaleinikoff; Editor: Earl Turner; Assistant Director: Charles S. Gould.

Cast: Buster Crabbe (Thunda/Capt. Roger Drum); Gloria Dea (Pha); Leonard Penn (Boris); Jack Ingram (Clark); Rusty Wescoatt (Kor); Nick Stuart (Degar); Rick Vallin (Andreov); Neyle Morrow (Nahee); Bart Davidson (Alexis); Alex Montoya (Lipah); Bernie Gozier (Zahlia); William Fawcett (High Priest); Lee Roberts (Blake); Frank Ellis (Ivan).

Chapter Titles: (1) Mission of Menace; (2) Red Shadows in the Jungle; (3) Into the Valley of Mist; (4) Thunda Meets His Match; (5) Thunda Turns the Tables; (6) Thunda's Desperate Chance; (7) Thunda Trapped; (8) Mission of Evil; (9) Menace of the Magnetic Rocks; (10) Lair of the Leopard; (11) An Ally From the Sky; (12) Riding Wild; (13) Red Raiders; (14) Savage Vengeance; (15) Judgement of the Jungle.

A jungle hero in the Tarzan mold, this adventure strip, one of the most beautifully drawn comics in the history of the medium, was created by writer Gardner Fox and artist Frank Frazetta; the strip premiered in THUNDA #1, published in April of 1952. The comic book itself far surpassed the Sam Katzman–produced Columbia serial starring Buster Crabbe.

TIFFANY JONES
newspaper strip

TIFFANY JONES (Cineworld, 1976)—theatrical feature; 90 minutes; color.

Credits: Producer and Director: Pete Walker; Screenplay: Alfred Shaughnessy; Music: Cyril Ornadel.

Cast: Anouska Hempel (Tiffany Jones); Ray Brooks; Eric Pohlmann; Martin Benson; Susan Sneers.

Created by writer Jerry Butterworth and artist Pat Tourret, this adventure strip about a fashionable '60s girl model premiered in November of 1964, distributed by Associated Newspapers, Ltd.

TILLIE THE TOILER
newspaper strip

TILLIE THE TOILER (Cosmopolitan/M-G-M, 1927)—theatrical feature; 6 reels.

Credits: Director: Hobart Henley; Screenplay: A. P. Younger (Original Story: Agnes Christine Johnston, Edward T. Lowe); Titles: Ralph Spence; Camera: William Daniels; Editor: Daniel J. Gray; Art Directors: Cedric Gibbons, David Townsend.

Cast: Marion Davies (Tillie Jones); Matt Moore (Mac); Harry Crocker (Pennington Fish); George Fawcett (Mr. Simpkins); George K. Arthur (Mr. Whipple); Estelle Clark (Sadie); Bert Roach (Bill); Gertrude Short (Bubbles); Clair McDowell (Maude Jones); Arthur Hoyt (Mr. Smythe).

This humor strip about a working girl was created by Russ Westover for King Features Syndicate and ran from January of 1921 to April of 1959.

TIM TYLER'S LUCK
newspaper strip

TIM TYLER'S LUCK (Universal, 1937)—theatrical serial; 12 chapters, approximately 20 minutes each.

TIM TYLER'S LUCK (Universal, 1937): A somewhat threadbare gorilla abducts Frances Robinson.

Credits: Associate Producers: Henry MacRae, Elmer Tambers; Directors: Forde Beebe, Wyndham Gittens; Screenplay: Wyndham Gittens, Ray Trampe, Norman S. Hall; Camera: Jerry Ash; Art Director: Ralph DeLacy; Supervising Editor: Saul A. Goodkind; Editors: Alvin Todd, Louis Todd, Joe Gluck.

Cast: Frankie Thomas (Tim Tyler); Frances Robinson (Lora Lacey); Al Shean (Professor Tyler); Norman Willis (Spider Webb); Earl Douglas (Lazarre); Jack Mulhall; Frank Mayo; Al Bridge; Pat O'Brien; William Benedict.

Chapter Titles: (1) Jungle Pirates; (2) Dead Man's Pass; (3) Into the Lion's Den; (4) The Ivory Trail; (5) Trapped in the Quicksands; (6) The Jaws of the Jungle; (7) The King of the Gorillas; (8) The Spider Caught; (9) The Gates of Doom; (10) A Race for Fortune; (11) No Man's Land; (12) The Kimberley Diamonds.

This jungle-adventure strip was created by Lyman Young for King Features Syndicate and ran from August of 1928 to July of 1972. The Universal serial is one of that studio's better cliffhanger efforts, made all the more appealing by its two charming leads, Frankie Thomas and Frances Robinson.

UP FRONT
newspaper strip

UP FRONT (Universal, 1951)—theatrical feature; 92 minutes.

Credits: Producer: Leonard Goldstein; Director: Alexander Hall; Screenplay: Stanley Roberts; Camera: Russell Metty; Music: Joseph Gershenson; Editor: Milton Carruth; Art Directors: Bernard Herzbrun, Alexander Golitzen.

Cast: David Wayne (Joe); Tom Ewell (Willie); Marina Berti (Emi); Jeffrey Lynn (Capt. Ralph Johnson); Richard Egan

(Capa); Maurice Cavell (Vuaglio); Vaughn Taylor (Major Lester); Silvio Minciotti (Peppa Rosso); Paul Harvey (Colonel Akeley); Roger De Koven (Sabatelli); Grazia Narciso (Signora Carvadossi); Tito Vuolo (Tarantino); Mickey Knox (Driver).

BACK AT THE FRONT (Universal, 1952)—theatrical feature; 87 minutes (*a.k.a.* WILLIE AND JOE BACK AT THE FRONT).

Credits: Producer: Leonard Goldstein; Director: George Sherman; Screenplay: Lou Breslow, Don McGuire, Oscar Brodney; Camera: Clifford Stine; Editor: Paul Weatherwax.

Cast: Tom Ewell (Willie); Harvey Lembeck (Joe); Mari Blanchard (Nida); Barry Kelley (General Dixon); Vaughn Taylor (Major Ormsby); Richard Long (Sergeant Rose); Russell Johnson (Johnny Redondo); Palmer Lee (Captain White); Aram Katcher (Ben); George Ramsey (Pete Wilson); Aen-Ling Chow (Sameko); Benson Fong (Rickshaw Boy).

Created by Bill Mauldin for the *45th Division News* U.S. Army paper, this humor strip about Willie and Joe, two forlorn G.I.'s, was picked up by the civilian press and was eventually distributed by United Features Syndicate, running until late 1945. It was revived briefly during the Korean war. The two film versions derived from Mauldin's characters are competent but unremarkable tripe.

THE VIGILANTE
comic book
National Periodicals/DC Comics

THE VIGILANTE (Columbia, 1947)—theatrical serial; 15 chapters, first chapter approximately 30 minutes, remaining chapters approximately 20 minutes each.

Credits: Producer: Sam Katzman; Director: Wallace Fox; Screenplay: George H. Plympton, Lewis Clay, Arthur Hoerl; Camera: Ira H. Morgan; Editor: Earl Turner; Music: Mischa Bakaleinikoff; Assistant Director: Mike Eason.

Cast: Ralph Byrd (The Vigilante/Greg Sanders); Ramsay Ames (Betty Winslow); Lyle Talbot (George Pierce); George Offerman, Jr. (Stuff); Robert Barron (Prince Hassan); Frank Marlo (Rabin); Hugh Prosser (Captain Reilly); Jack Ingram (Silver); Eddie Parker (Doc); George Chesebro (Walt); Bill Brauer (Thorne); Frank Ellis (Sadlow); Ed Cobb (Miller); Terry Frost (Lefty).

Chapter Titles (1) The Vigilante Rides Again; (2) Mystery of the White Horses; (3) Double Peril; (4) Desperate Flight; (5) In the Gorilla's Cage; (6) Battling the Unknown; (7) Midnight Rendezvous; (8) Blasted to Eternity; (9) The Fatal Flood; (10) Danger Ahead; (11) X–1 Closes In; (12) Death Rides the Rails; (13) The Trap that Failed; (14) Closing In; (15) The Secret of the Skyroom.

A western hero, The Vigilante premiered in ACTION COMICS #42 in 1943, and ran until the strip was discontinued in issue #201.

WONDER WOMAN
comic book
National Periodicals/DC Comics

WONDER WOMAN (ABC, 1974)—TV movie; 90 minutes; color.

Credits: Executive Producer: John D. F. Black; Producer: John G. Stephens; Director: Vincent McEveety; Screenplay: John D.

F. Black; Camera: Joseph Biroc; Art Director: Phil Bennett; Music: Artie Butler.

Cast: Cathy Lee Crosby (Wonder Woman/Diana Prince); Kaz Garas (Steve Trevor); Anitra Ford (Ahnjayla); Charlene Holt (The Queen Mother); Ricardo Montalban (Abner Smith); Andrew Prine (George Calvin); Donna Garrett (Cass); Robert Porter (Joey); Richard X. Slattery (Colonel); Ronald Long (Spender); Steven Mitchell (Thug); Sandy Gabiola (Ting); George Diaga (Captain); Beverly Gill (Dia); Jordan Rhodes (Bob).

WONDER WOMAN (ABC, 1975)—TV movie; 90 minutes; color.

Credits: Producer: Douglas S. Cramer; Director: Leonard J. Horn; Screenplay: Stanley Ralph Ross; Camera: Dennis Dalzell; Art Director: James Hulsey; Music: Charles Fox.

Cast: Lynda Carter (Wonder Woman/Diana Prince); Lyle Waggoner (Maj. Steve Trevor); John Randolph (Gen. Philip Blankenship); Cloris Leachman (The Queen Mother); Stella Stevens (Marcia); Red Buttons (Ashley Norman); Eric Braeden (Kapitan Drangel); Fannie Flagg (Amazon Doctor); Henry Gibson (Nicholas); Ken Mars (Colonel Von Balasko); Severn Darden (Villain).

WONDER WOMAN (ABC, CBS, 1976–79)—TV series; 60 episodes, 60 minutes each; color.

Credits: Executive Producers: Douglas S. Cramer, Wilfred Lloyd Baumes; Producers: Wilfred Lloyd Baumes, Charles B. Fitzsimmons, Mark Rodgers; Series Directors: Stuart Margolin, Bruce Bilson, Herb Wallerstein, Charles R. Rondeau, Richard Kinon, Leonard J. Horn, Alan Crosland, Jr., Barry Crane, Jack

WONDER WOMAN (CBS-TV, 1979): Lynda Carter.

Arnold, Robert Kelljan, Dick Moder, Leslie H. Martinson, Sigmund Neufeld, Jr., Gordon Hessler, Ivan Dixon, Don McDougall, Curtis Harrington, John Newland, Michael Caffey, Seymour Robbie; Series Writers: Bruce Kessler, David Ketchum, Margaret Armen, Ron Friedman, Jimmy Sangster, Paul Dubov, Gwen Bagni, Herb Berman, Elroy Schwartz, Tony Dimarco, Stephen Kandel, Skip Webster, Dallas Barnes, Judy Burns, Calvin Clements, Jr., Mark Rodgers, Brian McKay, Bruce Shelly, Richard Carr, Dan Ullman, Wilton Denmark, Anne Collins, S. S. Schweitzer, Tom Sawyer, Patrick Mathews, Dick Nelson, Dennis Landa, Alan Brennert, Katharyn Michaelian Powers, Kathleen Barnes, David Wise, Jackson Gillis, Michael McGreevey, Arthur Weingarten, John Gaynor, Bill Taylor, Glen Olson, Rod Baker, Robert Starke; Camera: Joe Jackman, Ric Wait, Ted Landon, Robert Hoffman; Art Directors: Frederick P. Hope, Phil Barber, Patricia Van Ryker; Music: Artie Kane, Charles Fox, Robert Prince, Richard La Salle, Johnny Harris, Angela Morley; Theme Music Vocals: The Charles Fox Singers.

Cast: Lynda Carter (Wonder Woman/Diana Prince); Lyle Waggoner (Maj. Steve Trevor/Steve Trevor, Jr.); Richard Eastham (General Blankenship); Normann Burton (Joe Atkinson); Cloris Leachman, Carolyn Jones, Beatrice Straight (The Queen Mother); Debra Winger (Drusilla); Beatrice Colen (Etta Candy); Pamela Susan Shoop (Magda); Erica Hagen (Dalma); Ed Begley, Jr. (Harold Farnum); Saundra Sharp (Eve); Judith Christopher (Beverly); Dulcie Jordan (Karen); Tom Kratochzil (Voice of Ira).

WONDER WOMAN was created not by a comic-book writer, but by psychologist William Moulton Marston (writing under the pseudonym "Charles Moulton"), who was also the inventor of the polygraph. Through this comic strip Marston sought to explore, in a positive way that children could understand, male-female relationships, a subject that wasn't exactly a primary concern in most comic books. Wonder

Woman made her initial appearance in ALL STAR COMICS #8 in 1941, and was awarded her own book immediately thereafter. The principal artist on these early strips was H. G. Peter. After an ineptly produced made-for-TV movie starring Cathy Lee Crosby, in which the character bore little resemblance to the comic book, visually or otherwise, a second TV version hit the mark, and was a far more faithful translation of the material. Starring an unknown actress named Lynda Carter, who began her career performing nude in a low-budget exploitation film, the series was done in a campy tongue-in-cheek style, but not overbearingly so, and Carter was the perfect flesh-and-blood embodiment of Wonder Woman. A period piece set in World War II, the series soon degenerated, though, and in the second season was updated to the present, with Wonder Woman becoming a government agent.

MISCELLANEOUS ENTRIES

THE FABULOUS FUNNIES (NBC, 1968)—TV special; 60 minutes; color.

Credits: Executive Producer: Lee Mendelson, Producer: George Schlatter; Director: Gordon Wiles; Screenplay: Bill Persky, Sam Denoff, Lee Mendelson; George Schlatter; Music: John Scott Trotter.

Cast: Carl Reiner (Host); Ken Berry; Jack Burns; Avery Schreiber.

Note: This program was rebroadcast in 1976.

THE FUNNY PAPERS (CBS, 1972)—TV special; 60 minutes; color.

Credits: Producer: Robert H. Precht; Director: John Moffitt; Screenplay: Gary Belkin; Music: Robert Arthur.

Cast: Raquel Welch (Little Orphan Annie/Brenda Starr/ Dragon Queen); Carroll O'Connor (Major Hoople/Daddy Warbucks); Jane Connell; Remak Ramsay; Bill Hinnant; Dorothy Emerson.

LEGENDS OF THE SUPERHEROES: CHALLENGE OF THE SUPERHEROES (NBC, 1979)—TV special; 60 minutes; color.

Credits: Producer and Director: William Carruthers; Associate Producer: Joel Stein; Costumes: Warden Neils; Stunts: Buddy Joe Hooker.

Cast: Adam West (Batman); Burt Ward (Robin); Rod Haase (Flash); Howard Murphy (Green Lantern); Garrett Craig (Captain Marvel); Barbara Joyce (Huntress); Danuta (Black Canary); Bill Nuckals (Hawkman); William Schallert (Red Cyclone/Retired Man); Frank Gorshin (Riddler); Mickey Morton (Solomon Grundy); Gabe Dell (Mordru); Charlie Callas (Sinestro); A'Lesia Brevard (Giganta); Howard Morris (Dr. Sivana/Weather Wizard).

LEGENDS OF THE SUPERHEROES: SUPERHEROES' ROAST (NBC, 1979)—TV special; 60 minutes; color.

Credits: Producer and Director: William Carruthers; Associate Producer: Joel Stein; Costumes: Warden Neils; Stunts: Buddy Joe Hooker.

Cast: Ed McMahon (Host); Adam West (Batman); Burt Ward (Robin); Alfie Wise (Atom); Ruth Buzzi (Aunt Minerva); Brad Sanders (Ghetto Man); Rod Haase (Flash); Howard Murphy

(Green Lantern); Garrett Craig (Captain Marvel); Barbara Joyce (Huntress); Danuta (Black Canary); Bill Nuckals (Hawkman); William Schallert (Red Cyclone/Retired Man); Frank Gorshin (Riddler); Mickey Morton (Solomon Grundy); Gabe Dell (Mordru); Charlie Callas (Sinestro); A'Lesia Brevard (Giganta); Howard Morris (Dr. Sivana/Weather Wizard).

THE FANTASTIC FUNNIES (CBS, 1980)—TV special; 60 minutes; color.

Credits: Producers: Lee Mendelson, Karen Crommie; Director: Lee Mendelson; Screenplay: Lee Mendelson; Camera: David Crommie; Music: Ed Bogas, Judy Munsen, Lee Mendelson.

Cast: Loni Anderson (Hostess); Keene Curtis; Patricia Patts; Howard Hesseman; Charles Schulz; Mort Walker; Hank Ketchum; Johnny Hart; Brad Anderson; Morrie Turner; Mel Lazarus; Russell Meyers; Dik Browne; Cathy Guisewite; Dean Young; John Raymond; John Cullen Murphy.

SUNDAY FUNNIES (NBC, 1983)—TV special; 60 minutes; color.

Credits: Executive Producer: Lee Mendelson; Producers: Frank Buxton, Jack Seifert; Director: Frank Buxton; Screenplay: Lee Mendelson, Gary Jacobs, Steven Michelle, Tom Moore, Jr., Marty Nadler, Bob Sand, Dennis Rinsler, Marc Warren; Music: Desarae Goyette, Tim Simon.

Cast: Loni Anderson (Hostess); Judith Cohen (Broomhilda); Dick Butkus (Tank McNamara); Milt Oberman (Crock); Paul Wilson (Frank); Martin Ferrero (Ernest); Ed Barth (Conrad); Murphy Dunne; Lois Faraker; Lisa Freeman; Desarae Goyette; Michael Harrington; Joanna Lee; Christopher Prince; Paul Ventura.

INDEX

Italicized numbers refer to pages with illustrations. Entries with the same title are differentiated by date (in chronological order) or format in parentheses.